T0135705

Studien zur Mustererkennung

herausgegeben von:

Prof. Dr.-Ing. Heinrich Niemann
Prof. Dr.-Ing. Elmar Nöth

Bibliografische Information der Deutschen Nationalbibliothek

Die Deutsche Nationalbibliothek verzeichnet diese Publikation in der Deutschen Nationalbibliografie; detaillierte bibliografische Daten sind im Internet über http://dnb.d-nb.de abrufbar.

ISBN 978-3-8325-4361-7
ISSN 1617-0695

Logos Verlag Berlin GmbH
Comeniushof
Gubener Str. 47
10243 Berlin
Tel.: +49 030 42 85 10 90
Fax: +49 030 42 85 10 92
INTERNET: http://www.logos-verlag.de

Analysis of Speech of People with Parkinson's Disease

Der Technischen Fakultät der
Universität Erlangen-Nürnberg

und

der Technischen Fakultät der
Universidad de Antioquia

zur Erlangung des Grades

DOKTOR-INGENIEUR

vorgelegt von

Juan Rafael Orozco-Arroyave

Erlangen — 2015

Deutscher Titel:

Sprachanalyse bei Menschen mit Parkinson-Krankheit

Als Dissertation genehmigt von der
Technischen Fakultät der
Friedrich-Alexander-Universität Erlangen-Nürnberg, Erlangen, Deutschland

und der

Technischen Fakultät der
Universidad de Antioquia, Medellín, Colombia

Tag der Einreichung:
Tag der Promotion:
Dekan:
Berichterstatter:

Prof. Dr.-Ing. habil. Elmar Nöth
Prof. Dr-Ing. Jesús Francisco Vargas-Bonilla

Acknowledgment

This thesis was developed during four years and many things can happen during this period of time, most of them were very happy, but some others were not. The most important is that during that time (and during all of my life), my family has been always with me, sharing successes and failures, supporting me. I would like to express my gratefulness and love to my parents, Luz Elena and Gustavo, without their continuous support this work would not have been possible. I am also very grateful to my brothers, Francisco and Gustavo. Specially Gustavo has been very close to me sharing successes and failures. Everybody in my family have shown to me the value and power of the patience and the perseverance.

I am very grateful to my advisors, Prof. Dr.-Ing. habil. Elmar Nöth and Prof. Dr.-Ing. Francisco Vargas. They gave me their support to address this work and their contributions helped to improve this thesis. Francisco has been not only my advisor during this work, but also my friend and my colleague during all this process. I want also to thank Elmar because he opened me the doors of the Speech Processing Group at Friedrich-Alexander-Universität, and since I came in Germany he has been like my father. His support and advice have been highly important to me and will lead most of the decisions for my future. His open mind and his selfless way to see the life made possible to develop this thesis between two institutions, Universidad de Antioquia in Colombia and Friedrich-Alexander-Universität in Germany.

I am also very grateful with the people (patients and volunteers) from Fundalianza Parkinson Colombia. Without their help and disposition to collaborate during the recording sessions, the development of this thesis would be impossible. Thank you my friends!

During the time I stayed in Germany I met a lot of people, particularly at the LME everybody was very friendly and open to talk and share free time with me. I would want to thank my colleagues in the Speech group, Florian, Tino, Caro, Fadi, Tobi, Stefan, and Korbinian. With all of them I had very nice conversations not only about speech processing, but also about politics, social problems, travels, jokes, and many other topics. Among them, I would want to express my deep gratitude to Tino and Florian, both helped me a lot with different technical and general things during my stays in Erlangen. With Tino I always had interesting and funny conversations, and his very detailed and precise way of reviewing contributed to improve this work. Florian was the person who fetched me at the Erlangen train station in my first visit to the city. He has been not only the person with whom I have discussed most of the experiments and results of this thesis, but also he has been like my brother in Germany. Every doubt I had was explained to me with a lot of patience, I never will forget his way of being so open and friendly, and I know that to visit him and his family will be one of the most important reasons for me to come again in Erlangen.

Besides the people in Erlangen, of course there are a lot of people in Medellín to whom I would want to express my gratefulness. Particularly the people from the speech group at GITA and SISTEMIC were essential during these four years. Elkyn, Camilo, Tatiana, Tomás, Nicanor, Brayan, Juan Manuel, etc, I wish to thank all of them for their patience and hard-working disposition.

I am also very grateful with Decireé, Johana, Camilo, Falco and "los muchachos". With their love and friendship it was much easier to overcome all of the challenges that the life put in front of me during these four years. Thanks to all!

There are also very close friends in Medellín that I would like to mention. Prof. Dr. Carlos Duque who is like my father in Universidad de Antioquia. He is a very successful researcher in Physics (Condensed Matter), he has inspired my desire to learn and also his advice helped me to understand the research activity as a profession. John Jairo, Lina Marcela, Caren, Juan Carlos Hoyos, and Víctor, have been the people that always accompanied me in the distance. Particularly, Hoyos and Víctor confirmed me on each beer we drank together, that have escaped from industry has been my best decision ever. Now I am working at Universidad de Antioquia, and every day I confirm that this is the best place to work worldwide. I am very grateful with my University because opened me the doors and provided me the serenity and confidence necessary to address my Ph.D.

Finally, I want to thank COLCIENCIAS for its financial support during the development of this thesis through the scholarship of the call # 528 "Generación del bicentenario 2011".

Erlangen, July 2015
Juan Rafael Orozco-Arroyave

Abstract

The analysis of speech of people with Parkinson's disease is an interesting and highly relevant topic that has been addressed in the research community during several years. There are important contributions of this topic considering perceptual and/or semi-automatic analyses. Those contributions are mainly based on detailed observations performed by clinicians; however, the automatic analysis of signals allowed by the rapid development of technological and mathematical tools, has motivated the research community to work on the development of computational tools to perform automatic analysis of speech. There are also several contributions on this topic; however, most of them are focused on sustained phonation of vowels and only consider recordings of one language. This thesis addresses two problems considering recordings of sustained phonations of vowels and continuous speech signals: (1) the automatic classification of Parkinson's patients vs healthy speakers, and (2) the prediction of the neurological state of the patients according to the motor section of the Unified Parkinson's Disease Rating Scale (UPDRS). The classification experiments are performed with recordings of three languages: Spanish, German, and Czech. German and Czech data were provided by other researchers, and Spanish data were recorded in Medellín, Colombia, during the development of this work. The analyses performed upon the recordings are divided into three speech dimensions: phonation, articulation, and prosody. Several classical approaches to assess the three speech dimensions are tested, and additionally a new method to model articulation deficits of Parkinson's patients is proposed. This new articulation modeling approach shows to be more accurate and robust than others to discriminate between Parkinson's patients and healthy speakers in the three considered languages. Additionally, the articulation and phonation seem to be the most suitable speech dimensions to predict the neurological state of the patients.

Kurzdarstellung

Die Analyse des Sprechens bei Personen mit der Parkinson-Krankheit ist ein interessantes und hochrelevantes Arbeitsfeld, mit dem sich die Forschung bereits seit einigen Jahren befasst. Es gibt bedeutende Beiträge auf diesem Gebiet, die perzeptive und/oder semiautomatische Analysen berücksichtigen. Diese Beiträge basieren hauptsächlich auf detaillierten Beobachtungen durch klinisches Personal. Die automatische Signalanalyse, die durch die schnelle Fortentwicklung technologischer und mathematischer Werkzeuge möglich geworden ist, hat die Forschungsgemeinde dazu motiviert, rechnergestützte Werkzeuge zur automatischen Sprechanalyse zu entwickeln. Auch hierfür gibt es bereits Publikationen; die meisten davon behandeln jedoch die gehaltene Phonation von Vokalen und berücksichtigen nur Aufnahmen in einer einzigen Sprache. Die vorliegende Arbeit befasst sich mit zwei Problemen, die Aufnahmen gehaltener Vokale und kontinuierlicher Sprachsignale betreffen: (1) die automatische Klassifikation von Parkinson-Patienten und gesunden Sprechern und (2) die Vorhersage des neurologischen Status der Patienten aufgrund des motorischen Teils des Unified Parkinson's Disease Rating Scale (UPDRS). Die Klassifikationsexperimente werden mit Aufnahmen aus drei Sprachen durchgeführt: Spanisch, Deutsch und Tschechisch. Die deutschen und tschechischen Sprachdaten wurden von anderen Forschern zur Verfügung gestellt, die spanischen Daten wurden in Medellín, Kolumbien, während der Arbeit an dieser Dissertation erhoben. Die Analysen der Aufnahmen werden gemäß dreier Dimensionen von Sprache aufgeteilt: Phonation, Artikulation und Prosodie. Verschiedene bekannte Ansätze zur Einschätzung der drei Dimensionen werden getestet. Zusätzlich wird eine neue Methode zur Modellierung der Artikulationsdefizite bei Parkinson-Patienten vorgeschlagen. Diese neue Aussprachemodellierung hat sich als genauer und robuster als andere Ansätze erwiesen, um zwischen Parkinson-Patienten und gesunden Sprechern in den drei betrachteten Sprachen zu differenzieren. Außerdem scheinen Artikulation und Phonation die geeignetsten Dimensionen zu sein, um den neurologischen Status der Patienten vorherzusagen.

Resumen

El análisis the voz en personas con enfermedad de Parkinson es un tema interesante y altamente relevante que ha sido abordado por la comunidad científica desde hace varios años. Existen contribuciones importantes en este tema considerando análisis de tipo perceptual y/o semi-automático. Estas contribuciones están basadas principalmente en observaciones detalladas que hacen los médicos; sin embargo, el rápido desarrollo de herramientas matemáticas y computacionales para el análisis automático de señales, ha motivado a la comunidad científica a desarrollar herramientas computacionales para el análisis automático de la voz. Existen también contribuciones en este tema; sin embargo, la mayoría de éstas están enfocadas en analizar fonaciones sostenidas de vocales considerando únicamente grabaciones en un idioma. Esta tesis aborda dos problemas considerando grabaciones de fonaciones sostenidas de vocales y señales de habla continua: (1) la clasificación automática de pacientes con enfermedad de Parkinson vs personas sanas, y (2) la predicción del estado neurológico de los pacientes de acuerdo con la sección de análisis motor de la escala UPDRS (por las siglas en Inglés de Unified Parkinson's Disease Rating Scale). Los experimentos de clasificación son realizados con grabaciones de tres idiomas: Español, Alemán, y Checo. Los datos en Alemán y Checho fueron proporcionados por otros investigadores, y las grabaciones en Español fueron realizadas en Medellín, Colombia, durante el desarrollo de esta tesis. Los análisis realizados con las grabaciones están divididos en tres dimensiones del habla: fonación, articulación, y prosodia. Se probaron varios enfoques clásicos para modelar las tres dimensiones y adicionalmente se propuso un nuevo método para modelar problemas articulatorios que se presentan en los enfermos con Parkinson. Este nuevo enfoque para modelar articulación muestra ser más preciso y robusto que los demás para discriminar entre personas con enfermedad de Parkinson y personas sanas en los tres idiomas considerados. Adicionalmente, la articulación y la fonación muestran ser las dimensiones más apropiadas para predecir el estado neurológico de los pacientes.

Contents

Chapter 1

Introduction

1.1. Motivation

Neurological diseases affect millions of people around the world. Particularly, Parkinson's disease (PD) affects about 2% of people older than 65 years [Rijk 00]. PD is a neurological disorder that alters functions of the basal ganglia and it is characterized by the progressive loss of dopaminergic neurons in the substantia nigra of the midbrain [Horn 98]. PD has significant impacts in the social, psychological, and physical interaction of patients. The problems induced by PD include motor deficits such as bradykinesia, rigidity, postural instability, and resting tremor. Non-motor deficits include negative effects on sensory system, sleep, behavior, cognition, and emotion [Loge 78]. According to the Royal College of Physicians in London[1] [Nati 06], in order to relieve such impact, in addition to the pharmacological treatment, PD patients should have access to a set of services and therapies including specialized nursing care, physiotherapy, and *speech and language therapy* [Wort 13]. The cost of PD-related treatment per patient exceeds $US 4,072 in USA just during the first year after the diagnosis. When the ambulatory assistance (which is typically required in advanced-state patients) is considered, the cost could be around $US 26,467 in the same period of time [John 13b]. Assuming that the patients live about 12 years after the diagnosis, such economical burden during this period of time could be decreased in about $US 60,657 if the disease progression is slowed in at least 20% [John 13a]. On the other hand, it is estimated that 90% of PD patients develop speech impairments, however only between 3% and 4% of them receive speech therapy [Rami 08]. The average age of diagnosis of PD is 60 years and affected patients often become disabled or retire early due to their motor, cognition and/or speech impairments [Alve 05].

There is a great interest in the research community to develop methods to assess and improve the communication ability of PD patients. Most of the approaches have considered sustained phonations for the analysis i.e., uttering a vowel during several seconds. This kind of evaluation allows assessing the phonation capability of a patient, which is basically the ability to produce air in the lungs and use it to make the vocal folds vibrate to produce vocal sounds. However, it is well known that the speech production includes many other processes involving the movement of several limbs and muscles to produce

---

[1]https://www.rcplondon.ac.uk/
Last retrieved 7/2/2015.

intelligible utterances. According to the Parkinson's Disease Foundation[2], due to the lack of motor control, the communication skills of PD patients are highly impacted and even in the most advanced stages the patients become extremely unintelligible. In the light of the effects and prevalence of the speech disorders in PD patients, it is necessary to develop methodologies for the automatic evaluation of speech considering different subsystems involved in its production process such as phonation, articulation, and prosody. Additionally, such methodologies and their derived technologies should be able to assess speech spoken in different languages and recording conditions i.e., microphones, sound cards, and different acoustic conditions, thus maximizing their impact on the society. This thesis addresses the problem of modeling speech signals of people with PD in order to detect the disease and to predict the neurological state of the patients. Three databases with recordings in three different languages are considered. The main contribution of this thesis comprises the accurate modeling of the difficulties exhibited by PD patients to start and to stop motor activities. Those difficulties are modeled from speech by considering the instant when the vocal fold vibration starts or stops.

1.2.   State-of-the-art

The speech can be studied including several characteristics and subsystems involved in its production. Particularly the speech of people with Parkinson's disease has been studied considering phonation, articulation, respiration, prosody, and resonance. In order to give a general and complete view of the different phenomena involved in Parkinson's speech, studies that consider these aspects of speech are reviewed in this section. Contributions to the speech analysis and therapy in PD patients considering the Medical and Engineering approaches have been included. Those studies that considered either observation or statistical significance tests to conclude regarding different phenomena in speech of PD patients were included into the group of Medical contributions. The studies that used statistical learning methods, pattern recognition techniques, or machine learning methods to discriminate between PD and HC speakers were included into the group of Engineering contributions. The main purpose of this section is to give the reader a complete view of the advances in the topic from both approaches. Although Parkinson's disease affects several functions of the body, this review is restricted to studies in speech analysis.

PD was first described by James Parkinson in 1817 [Park 17]. The motor problems observed by the author include resting tremor, abnormal gait, paralysis, and loss of muscle strength. Besides, James Parkinson described several speech impairments developed by PD patients. Although the early observed impact of PD in the patients speech, the interest of the research community to understand and/or correct such impact is relatively recent [Darl 69]. The first approach was focused on describing perceptual characteristics of the Parkinsonian speech [Cant 63, Cant 65a, Cant 65b]. Several symptoms were associated to hypokinetic dysarthria including monopitch, reduced stress, mono-loudness, imprecise consonants, inappropriate silences, among others. The first observations and studies were focused on the phonation and articulation subsystems of speech, for instance the imprecise production of stop consonants such as /p/, /t/, /k/, /b/, and /g/, were observed by Logemann

---

[2]http://www.pdf.org/en/speech_problems_pd
Last retrieved 7/2/2015.

et al. in [Loge 81]. The authors associated such behavior to an inadequate tongue elevation. Lack of changes in the speech intensity during the production of stop consonants was also reported. Other studies consider the clinical description of speech impairments and their relation with other biological processes such as swallowing and respiration. In [Robb 86] the authors observed the movement patterns in the larynx of PD patients during swallowing. The speech production was also analyzed using videofluoroscopy of 6 patients with PD and 6 age-matched healthy controls (HC). All of the patients exhibited abnormal oropharyngeal movements and timing. The duration of the velar movements during speech production was different in PD patients with respect to the HC. Articulation deficits in consonant sounds such as /k/, /g/, /f/, /v/, /s/, and /z/, were also observed.

In order to delay the impact of PD in voice, Ramig et al. proposed the Lee-Silverman Voice Treatment (LSVT®) [Rami 88], which is an auto-therapy guide seeking to improve the voice quality of PD patients [King 94, Rami 94]. Details of the speech tasks included in this guide are provided in Section 2.4.1. Additionally, the speech and gestures of different areas in the face of PD patients while speaking are perceptually studied via kinematic and acoustic semi-automatic evaluations performed by Forrest et al. in [Forr 89]. The authors considered a total of 17 participants, 9 PD patients and 8 age-matched HC. The speakers were asked to pronounce 6 sentences 25 times. The acoustic analysis consisted on temporal measures of the voice onset time (VOT) and the onsets of formant transitions, defined as a minimum of 20 Hz change over a 20 ms interval [Weis 88]. The kinematic analysis was performed by measuring the movements of the inferior and superior lips and jaw. The perceptual evaluation was performed by four speech/language pathologists which scaled the severity of the dysarthria perceived on each sentence in an arbitrary scale that ranges between 0 and 100. The labels assigned by the specialists to each speaker were averaged to rank the participants. According to the authors observations, opening gestures, jaw displacements, and velocities are about half with respect to those produced by the HC speakers. Reduced duration of vocalic segments and transitions, and increased VOT were also observed. Finally, the authors claimed that the observed impairments increase with the disease severity. On the other hand, several articulatory deficits suffered by people with PD were documented by Ackerman et al. [Acke 91]. The authors considered speech recordings of 12 speakers with PD and 12 HC. The recordings were sampled at 20 kHz and manually segmented. The set of features extracted from the speech recordings includes sound pressure level (SPL) in stop consonants such as /b/, /g/, /p/, and /k/, and the mean syllable duration (MSD) defined as the time interval between syllabic peaks in the SPL contour measured on different consonant-vowel words. The intensity during closure (IDC) and the transition quotient (TQ) were also measured. IDC is measured on the two stop consonants preceding and following a stressed target vowel of a test word, and TQ is the quotient between the movement portion of a syllable and the full syllable duration. The movement portion is defined as the 5% of the time during rising or falling the SPL in a consonant. The authors reported a reduction of the articulatory precision in stop consonants produced by PD patients while the speech tempo did not differentiate between PD and HC speakers. The authors stated that the patients compensate their low speech rate by producing movements with reduced amplitude in the articulators e.g., lips, tongue, velum, and jaw. Other phenomena related with the abnormal phase closure and phase asymmetry in the larynx of PD patients were observed in [Pere 96]. The authors performed visual-perceptual ratings of endoscopic and stroboscopic examinations of 22 patients with PD and 7 with Parkinson'splus[3]. Besides the abnormal closure pattern, the authors reported the presence of vertical laryngeal tremor in more than 55% of the PD patients. In the same way, the phonation patterns in the speech of PD patients are studied in [Jime 97]. The fundamental frequency of speech (F_0) and its variation in amplitude and frequency i.e., shimmer and jitter respectively, along with the harmonics to noise ratio (HNR) and other phonatory measurements are considered. The authors evaluated 22 untreated PD patients i.e., not treated with dopaminergic drugs, and 28 HC. All of the participants were native Spanish speakers and they were asked to repeat the sustained vowel /a/ three times and to read a sentence. The sustained phonations were sampled at 20 kHz while the sentence was sampled at 10 kHz. The authors observed higher jitter and shimmer in the patients speech than in the controls. Conversely, HNR and F_0 were lower in PD patients. These observations were confirmed later by the authors considering a set of 41 PD patients who were under dopaminergic treatment [Gamb 97]. Besides the periodicity and noise measures, the aerodynamics of phonation in PD patients is studied in [Jack 99]. The authors reported abnormal muscular function in the larynx of PD patients during phonation. The aerodynamics parameters considered in the study include laryngeal resistance (LR), sub-glottal pressure (SGP), aerodynamic power (AePw), and vocal efficiency (VE). A total of 24 patients with PD and 17 HC were asked to pronounce the sustained vowel /a/ at different intensity levels, 75 dB, 80 dB, and 85 dB. The intensity level was controlled using visual feedback for the speakers. The experiments were performed using a device equipped with a balloon-type valve that closes the outflow while the speaker is producing the sustained phonation.

In addition to the impairments in phonation and articulation, problems in the prosody of PD patients have been observed as well. In [Le D 98] the authors studied the differences in the prosody of 10 patients with PD, 10 with Friedreich's ataxia, and 20 HC speakers. The participants were asked to pronounce several sentences including questions and statements. Voiced frames of the speech recordings were manually segmented and the F_0 contour was measured. The authors concluded that healthy speakers produce questions with higher F_0 in the last syllable with respect to the F_0 in other syllables. Such difference is not observed in the patients with PD or Friedreich's ataxia. Reduced variability of F_0 is also observed in the sentences uttered by the patients. Further to the impairments in prosody, sometimes the PD patients also show repetitive speech phenomena, affecting the fluency of their speech. This behavior is documented by Benke et al. in [Benk 00]. The authors analyzed 53 patients, 24 in advanced-state and 29 in mid-state. Six speech tasks were evaluated including spontaneous speech, answering of questions, description of a picture, read text, and repetition of 15 words and 4 sentences. The speech recordings were analyzed word by word in order to count the number of repetitions. 15 of the patients showed repetitive speech, most of them from the advanced-state group. Two different types of repetitive phenomena were observed (i) hyper-fluent, which is the increasing speech rate, often poorly articulated and occasionally decreasing loudness, and (ii) dys-fluent, characterized by a constant speech rate, well articulated, and with constant loudness.

Aside from phonation, articulation, and prosody, respiration is also an important aspect of speech production that is affected in PD patients [Robb 86]. Bearing in mind that phonation is mainly associated to the ability of producing air in the lungs to make the vocal folds vibrate to produce vocal sounds, one could think that making therapy to improve either of these two aspects, phonation or respiration, there would be benefits in the patient's voice.

---

[3]It is an atypical variant of Parkinson's disease that induces motor impairments also.

However, in 2001 Ramig et al. [Rami 01] compared the effectiveness of the LSVT® with respect to the respiratory therapy (RET). A total of 33 PD patients were considered, 21 of them were in the LSVT® program and the other 12 were in the RET program. After two years of having performed the LSVT® treatment, the patients showed improvements in their vocal function, while the group in the RET program did not show such improvements. One of the reasons given by the authors to explain this difference is because the evaluated treatments have different emphasis, thus the results should be reflected in different functions. This result indicates that although both processes, phonation and respiration, are related, the therapies to improve them should be different and specific to each aspect.

Another aspect of speech, which is important to pronounce some consonant and vocal sounds correctly, is the resonance. This characteristic is also impaired in PD patients and typically it is manifested as an excess of air in the nasal cavity i.e., hypernasality. This impairment appears due to slow movement and rigidity of the muscles involved in the velopharyngeal mechanism [Duff 95]. Further studies performed by Duffy et al. indicate that hypernasality may be present in Parkinsonian speech, however it is not prominent [Duff 00].

Further prosodic and articulatory aspects of PD speech are studied by Goberman et al. in [Gobe 05]. The authors analyzed several acoustic differences between conversational and "clear" speech in 12 individuals with PD. The evaluation considered three speech tasks, (1) the series of /h/ + vowel + /d/ (hVd) tokens embedded in the phrase "say hVd again". The included vowels were /i/, /u/, /a/, /æ/, (2) reading of the first paragraph in the 'rainbow passage' [Fair 60], and (3) 2 minutes of monologue. The authors defined conversational speech as utterances pronounced by the patients at their normal tone and loudness, and clear speech as utterances pronounced paying special attention of the clearness i.e., there was one person indicating when an utterance is not clear enough. The authors observed lower articulation rate, measured in syllables per second, in clear speech than in conversational one. The mean value of F_0 and its variability were higher in clear speech recordings. The authors also observed that the patients make more pauses in monologues than in read texts. The first two formants, F_1 and F_2, are extracted from the four vowels in the hVd tokens to build the vocal quadrilateral in the F_1-F_2 space. The area of such quadrilateral was calculated to infer the tongue position during the production of corner vowels [Turn 95]. Although the findings were not statistically significant, the authors concluded that it appears that individuals with PD have a deficit in vowel area i.e., produce vowels with decreased tongue excursions. A different approach for the analysis of articulation and prosodic aspects in the speech of PD patients is presented by Skodda et al. in [Skod 08]. The authors considered a total of 121 people with PD and 70 HC. The analysis was performed in the first and the last sentence of a 170-syllabic text. Articulatory and speech rates were calculated measuring the length of each syllable and the pauses at the end of each word and within polysyllabic words. The authors defined several duration-related features, such as total speech time (TST), which is the total duration of the utterance, total pause time (TPT), defined as the time of all pauses in the utterances (the authors defined pauses as silences longer than 10 ms), net speech time (NST), defined as TST-TPT, time and number of pauses withing polysyllabic words and at the end of the words, percentage pause time (Pinw%), defined as the pause time within polysyllabic words divided by TPT, total speech rate (TSR) defined as syllables per second relative to TST, net speech rate (NSR), defined as syllables per second relative to the NST, and articulatory acceleration

(AA), defined as the difference of NSR measured on the last and the first sentences. The authors observed higher AA in PD patients than in HC. They also observed that the patients make less but longer pauses at the end of words and less pauses withing polysyllabic words. The authors conclude that there are impaired rhythm and timing in the speech of people with PD. These rhythm impairments were confirmed in [Skod 10]. In this study the authors analyzed several duration-based measures in recordings of the repetition of the syllables /pa/ and /ba/. A total of 73 patients with PD and 43 HC were recorded. According to the results, the average duration of the first four repetitions of the syllables is longer in the patients while the variability of the duration of the 5th and 20th repetition is lower. Articulatory aspects in PD speech and how do they are affected by lexical factors in read words are considered in [Wats 08]. 10 patients with PD and 10 healthy speakers were evaluated. The participants uttered three times a total of 32 consonant-vowel-consonant (CVC) words. The speech recordings were sampled at 44.1 kHz with 16-bit resolution. Four subsets with 8 words each are formed according to their frequency of use (high/low use) and their phonological neighborhoods (high/low densities). The vowels /i/, /u/, /a/, and /æ/ were semi-automatically segmented from the words using Praat [Boer 01]. F_1 and F_2 values in Bark scale are extracted to form a vowel space in the F_1-F_2 plane [Gobe 05]. The vowel space dispersion is calculated with the Euclidean distance measured from each vowel to the center of the vowel space. The authors reported contracted vowel space dispersion in PD patients. The frequency of use and the phonological neighborhood did not provided enough information to discriminate between PD and HC speakers.

Changes in F_0 and the onset of voicing in patients with PD is studied by Goberman et al. in [Gobe 08]. The authors present a study of the short-term phonatory behavior in individuals with PD. They measured F_0 at the offset and onset of phonation, before and after a voiceless consonant. The dataset considered for this study consisted of 9 patients with PD and 8 HC. The speech of the patients was recorded in both, OFF-state (30 minutes before taking medication in the morning) and On-state (1 hour after the medication in the morning). The days of the recordings in ON- and OFF-states were different. The participants were asked to read twice the first paragraph of the 'rainbow passage' [Fair 60]. The recordings were analyzed using the software CSL-4400 of Kay Elemetrics. The analyses were performed with the two words "one finds" within the sentence "people look, but no *one finds* it". The reasons for the authors to take this portion of the read text were, (1) these words are entire voiced with the only exception in the consonant /f/, (2) the voiced segments are long enough to perform phonation analysis, and (3) this portion of the text was read in a relatively natural context. Acoustic measurements were taken on the phonatory offset, which consisted on 10 periods of vocal folds vibration before the consonant /f/. The same analysis takes place on the phonatory onset, which consisted on 10 cycles after the consonant /f/. F_0 and its variability are measured on phonatory onset and offset. According to their observations, the authors concluded that people with PD have problems producing rapid offset of voicing, and the possible compensatory adjustment for such problems is to start the phonatory offset gesture earlier than the healthy speakers. Similarly, patients in OFF-state appear to start voicing earlier than those in ON-state of medication. Differences in the laryngeal tension and aerodynamic factors are also observed in PD patients compared to the HC speakers. Further to the aforementioned analysis, the authors remarked the existence of contradictory reports regarding the VOT measured on people with PD i.e., there are studies reporting values of VOT higher in PD patients than in HC [Weis 84], but there are also studies reporting lower VOT values in PD patients [Forr 89]. The authors stated that further research about VOT is required to clarify which is the most recurrent behavior in speech of people with PD. In that way, the time to initiate speech was studied by Walsh et al. in [Wals 11]. The authors analyzed the influence of increased syntactic complexity and utterance length on speech production and comprehension of people with PD. A total of 6 sentences read 15 times by 16 patients with PD and 16 HC were considered. Both, speech and video signals were recorded. The lip aperture (LA) was measured from the videos in order to analyze the coordination of the upper and lower lips, and the jaw to control the oral opening during phonation. According to the results, the patients take longer time to initiate speech and also make more mistakes on the speaking tasks. The syntactic complexity and length of the sentences affected in the same extent both groups of speakers, PD and HC.

Recent the contributions in the Medical field have been mainly focused on the prosody and articulation analyses. Sapir et al., [Sapi 10] proposed the formant centralization ratio (FCR) as a new measure to assess articulation in dysarthric speech. The authors evaluated 38 patients with PD and 14 HC considering different spectral features such as VSA, natural logarithm of VSA, and the quotient F_{2i}/F_{2u}, where F_{2i} and F_{2u} are the values of the second formants extracted from the vowels /i/ and /u/, respectively. All of the participants were native English speakers, and were asked to repeat three sentences several times per day during at least 2-3 days before and after receiving voice treatment based on the LSVT[®] [Rami 88]. The set of three sentences included (1) "the blue spot is on the key", (2) "the potato stew is in the pot", and (3) "the stew pot is packed with peas". The vowels /a/, /i/, and /u/ were extracted from the recordings to perform the analyzes. According to the reported results, FCR and F_{2i}/F_{2u} are highly correlated ($r = -0.90$) and both can differentiate between dysarthric and non-dysarthric speech signals. Further, in [Skod 11c], Skodda et al. analyzed the influence of PD in vowel articulation and its correlation with a measure of speech rate and the F_0 variability. The authors considered recordings of 68 patients (34 male and 34 female) and 32 HC (16 male and 16 female). The participants read a set with four sentences. To exclude difficulties in reading, the participants read the text twice and the second sequence was taken for the analysis. The vowel articulation was evaluated with the vowel articulation index (VAI) and the triangular vowel space area (tVSA) which were extracted from the vowels /a/, /i/, and /u/. The speech rate was analyzed by means of the NSR [Skod 08]. The measurements were performed using the software Praat [Boer 01]. The authors concluded that VAI values are reduced in male and female PD patients, while tVSA was only reduced in male PD patients. They did not found correlation between the extent of the disease and the considered vowel articulation features. The authors reported also a significant reduction of the F_0 variability in the course of reading. This finding was validated later in [Skod 11b] when the authors compared this feature measured from the last sentence with respect to the measure in the first one. Regarding the effect of the dopaminergic therapy in speech, according to the findings reported in [Skod 11b], the effect of the levodopa admission in speech is still inconclusive. Also in 2011, the same group of authors studied different prosodic parameters in a larger group of patients [Skod 11a]. 169 speakers with PD and 64 HC red the same set of sentences considered in [Skod 11c]. Correlations between several prosodic features and the gender were explored. According to the results, the variability of F_0 in male and female patients is reduced compared to HC. A reduction in the perceptual pause time within polysyllabic words was observed in PD patients. No correlations were found between intonation and articulatory rate. VAI and tVSA were again studied by the same authors in [Skod 12]. Further to the analysis of statistical differences of the VAI and tVSA values, the authors studied possible correlations between the measures and the motor score of the unified Parkinson's disease rating scale (UPDRS) [Move 03], which is widely used by neurologists to subjectively quantify the disease progression. As the articulation measures considered by the authors do not show correlation with the scale, the authors concluded that impairments in vowel articulation and the progressive prosodic alterations could be the result of an escalation of axial dysfunction that is too subtle to be mirrored by the UPDRS motor score.

On the other hand, possible differences in the impact of the lateralization of basal ganglia dysfunction in speech of PD patients is studied in [Flas 12]. The authors considered a total of 60 patients with PD, 30 with predominant symptoms on the left-side and 30 on the right-side. 40 healthy speakers were also included in the study. The participants performed the repetition of the syllable /pa/ and read a text. Several prosodic features related to speech rate, duration, and onset, among others, were extracted from the recordings. According to the results, syllable repetition is significantly more instable in both groups of PD patients than in the HC. However, the patients with more affection in the left-side showed higher pace and further significant acceleration. This finding suggests that lateral basal ganglia dysfunction differentially affects the stability of syllable repetition pace.

The progression of the speech impairments due to PD is analyzed in a longitudinal study presented in [Skod 13]. A total of 80 patients with PD and 60 healthy speakers were considered. Both groups of participants were tested and retested after at least 12 months (average time interval: 32.5 months). The speakers were asked to read a text with four phonetically balanced sentences. The sustained phonation of the vowel /a/ was also recorded. Four "speech modalities" were evaluated with different measurements, (1) voice: considering jitter, shimmer, HNR, and mean of F_0 measured on the sustained phonation, (2) articulation: considering VAI, and the percentage of pauses withing polysyllabic words (Pinw%), (3) fluency: considering NSR, and the pause ratio, and (4) prosody: considering the variability of F_0. The recordings were also perceptually evaluated by two neurologists who were blinded for the speakers' condition. The score of each patient was assigned according to a four-dimensional scoring system that is used in the Department of Neurology at the Ruhr-University of Bochum in Germany. Such scale is used for the clinical description of dysarthria and considers the same speech modalities that were objectively measured. The overall intelligibility was also perceptually scored in an scale with four levels: "good", "fair", "moderate", and "poor". When the speech signals of the first and the second recording session were compared, significant differences were found in shimmer, HNR, NSR, Pinw%, and VAI. The acoustic features reveled that the speech deterioration in PD patients correlates with the progression of the disease. The authors highlight that the combination of perceptual and acoustic features allows performing clinical analyses of different modalities of speech and also analyzing objective measures of individual variables reflecting changes that could be too subtle to be detected perceptually. Although the findings are promising, the authors claim that further research is necessary to state appropriate methods of speech investigations which produce objective data, fulfill the demands of validity and reproducibility, time and cost effectiveness, and mirror best the functional disability of patients.

Note that the Medical contributions report observed phenomena in PD speech mainly based on statistical significance tests. However, such analysis is not sufficient to give a complete picture of the extent to which a set of measures is useful in determining impairments in PD speech [Hube 00]. Methods of statistical learning theory, pattern recognition, and machine learning, have been used in the literature in order to measure the extent to which people with PD can be discriminated from HC. In the following of this section, several studies considering such statistical learning methods to discriminate PD and HC speakers are reviewed.

As in the Medical field, one of the earliest approaches in the studies from the Engineering field was focused on the analysis of phonation. In 2009, Little et al. [Litt 09] considered a set with 23 PD patients and 8 HC. Each speaker produced the sustained vowel /a/ about six times. The authors calculated different dysphonia features to discriminate between people with PD and HC. The authors use Praat [Boer 01] to calculate the set of measurements which includes two versions of jitter (absolute and average absolute difference between cycles), the amplitude perturbation quotient (APQ), shimmer, HNR, and noise to harmonics ratio (NHR), among others. Along with the "classical" measures, the authors estimate four features which are derived from the nonlinear analysis of speech. The set of nonlinear measures includes recurrence period density entropy (RPDE) [Litt 07], detrended fluctuation analysis (DFA) [Litt 07], correlation dimension (D2) [Oroz 13b], and the pitch period entropy (PPE), which is a novel measure of dysphonia introduced in [Litt 09]. Additionally, the authors performed an exhaustive search through the set of features in order to find the most discriminative subset of measures. After such search the subset of features included HNR, RPDE, DFA, and PPE. The authors discriminate between PD and HC speakers using a support vector machine (SVM) with Gaussian kernel. The SVM was trained following a bootstrap re-sampling strategy with 50 replicates [Hast 01]. The authors reported an overall correct classification performance of 91.4%. One year later Sakar and Kursun in [Saka 10] considered the same set of recordings of [Litt 09]. The authors calculated a total of 22 features including those considered by Little et al., and two additional nonlinear measures of the fundamental frequency variation. The authors used also a SVM to discriminate between PD and HC speakers. In this study the SVM was trained following a leave-one-speaker-out cross-validation (LOSO-CV) strategy. Additionally, the authors show that there is a bias in the validation strategy addressed in [Litt 09], since in the bootstrap re-sampling method, several recordings of the test set are also included in the train set. The accuracy reported using the set of features selected by Sakar et al., and training the SVM with LOSO-CV is around 81.5%, while validating with bootstrap it increased up to 92.8%. Finally, the authors tested the same set of features included in [Litt 09] and reported accuracies of 91.4% and 65.1% with bootstrap and LOSO-CV, respectively. Further to highlighting the importance of avoiding over-fitting in the validation procedure, the authors claim that voice measures have a clear potential for PD evaluation. Also in 2010, the impact of the progression of PD in the voice of the patients is analyzed in [Tsan 10a] and [Tsan 11]. The authors considered sustained phonations of the vowel /a/ produced by 42 PD patients. The speakers were recorded several times during 6 months. A total of 5923 recordings were included in the study i.e., about 141 repetitions per patient. The recordings were captured with the device presented in [Goet 09]. The set of features calculated is the same of those considered in [Litt 09]. The patients were evaluated three times during the study, at the beginning of the program, and after three and six months. The patients were labeled according to the UPDRS motor scale on each evaluation. The authors mapped the UPDRS values using two regression techniques, classification and regression trees (CART) and random forest (RF). The validation strategy was 10-folds cross-validation, i.e., 90% of the recordings are randomly chosen for training and the remaining 10% for testing. The process is repeated 100 times to estimate the performance of the system. Note that in this study each speaker repeated the phonation about 141 times, thus the speaker independence is not guaranteed in the experiments, leading to possible biased and over-optimistic results. Additionally, the authors reported about 2 UPDRS points difference from the clinician's estimates ($p < 0.001$); however it is not reported in the papers any trivial estimator of the UPDRS scale in order to have a direct comparison point relative to the performance of the system. A similar methodology but applied to perform automatic discrimination of speakers with PD and HC is addressed in [Tsan 12]. The authors evaluated phonation of people with PD considering 132 features extracted from sustained phonations of the English vowel /a/. A total of 263 voice samples were recorded from 43 subjects (33 with PD and 10 HC). The set of measures included different estimations of jitter and shimmer, several variants of noise measures, mel-frequency cepstral coefficients (MFCCs), and nonlinear measures. This set of features is described in [Tsan 10b]. The authors applied four different feature selection techniques to find the best subset of features that separates between phonations of PD patients and HC. A 10-fold CV strategy was followed to perform the selection of features. The final subset of features comprises a total of ten measures which are selected applying a voting scheme over the result of each feature selection technique. Two different classification strategies are compared, RF and SVM with Gaussian kernel. The CV process is repeated 100 times randomly permuting the subsets prior to splitting into train and test. Errors over the 100 repetitions are averaged. The authors reported accuracies ranging between 94.4% and 98.6% depending on the feature selection technique. Note that as in [Litt 09, Tsan 10a, Tsan 11], each speaker repeated the task several times and the train and test subsets are formed randomly, without guarantee of speaker independence (or at least not reported by the authors). According to the validation methodologies for automatic classification systems, train and test subsets must be separated during all of the experiment. Additionally, the validation process must be speaker-independent to avoid bias and to find more realistic results [Saen 06]. This methodological issue can lead to optimistic results and possible biased conclusions. In particular, since the target (the detection of PD) is constant per speaker, there is a chance for the system to decide by recognizing the speaker rather than recognizing the pathology.

Phonation, articulation, and prosody subsystems of speech were analyzed by Rusz et al. in [Rusz 11]. The authors considered recordings from 46 native Czech speakers, 23 with PD and 23 HC. The voice recordings comprise six different tasks including (1) isolated vowels pronounced in a sustained manner, (2) rapid repetition of the syllables /pa-ta-ka/, also called diadochokinetic (DDK) evaluation, (3) reading of a text with 136 words, (4) one monologue of at least 90 seconds, (5) reading of sentences, and (6) rhythmically reading of a text with 34 words (8 rhymes followed by an example given by the examiner). Phonation features were evaluated on sustained vowels and the set of measures includes the variation of F_0, different versions of jitter and shimmer, and the noise content quantified using HNR and NHR. The evaluation of articulation was mostly performed considering the DDK task, and the set of features includes the number of vocalizations of /pa-ta-ka/ per second, the ability to maintain a constant rate of consonant-vowel combinations in the pronunciation of /pa-ta-ka/, and different spectral-based measures of energy. Additionally, the authors included the VSA measured from the sustained phonation of the vowels /a/, /i/, and /u/

[Sapi 10]. The evaluation of prosody was performed considering read texts, sentences, and the monologue. The set of prosody features includes the variation of F_0, percent pause time, articulation rate, number of pauses, standard deviation of the intensity, and the ability to reproduce perceived rhythm. The authors reported that 78% of the patients evidenced speech problems; articulation is the second most affected dimension of speech while prosody was the most affected even in the initial-state of the disease. The authors also found that the variation of F_0 measured on the monologues and emotional sentences contains information that could be used in separating HC from PD speakers. Phonation, articulation, and prosody modeling are also considered by Bocklet et al. in [Bock 13]. A total of 176 native German speakers were recorded, 88 with PD and 88 HC. Articulation modeling is performed using the 13 MFCCs along with their first and second order derivatives, forming a feature vector with 39 components per voice frame. The feature vectors per speaker are modeled using a Gaussian Mixture Model (GMM), following a Universal Background Modeling strategy. The GMM is created using a total of 128 Gaussians trained on the whole training set using the Expectation-Maximization (EM) algorithm. The means of the UBM are adapted by relevance Maximum A Posteriori (MAP) adaptation to find specific mixtures per speaker. Finally, the means of each Gaussian are used as speaker-specific features, forming 4992-dimensional (128×39) feature vectors per speaker. The prosodic modeling is performed with the Erlangen prosody module [Zeis 06]. The features are derived from F_0, energy, duration, pauses, jitter, and shimmer, among others. Feature vectors are formed computing mean, minimum, maximum, and standard deviation of a total of 73 features per voiced segment (292-dimensional). The phonation modeling is based on the estimation of physical parameters of the glottis. A two-mass vocal fold model is used with the aim of finding physically meaningful parameters [Stev 98]. A total of 9 parameters are derived from the model. Additionally, a set of 1582 acoustic features are extracted using the openSMILE toolkit [Eybe 10]. The experiments are performed with recordings of 176 native German speakers, 88 with PD and 88 HC. The set of speech tasks comprises spontaneous speech, read text, read sentences, isolated words, sustained vowels, and the repetition of the syllable /pa/. The discrimination between PD and HC speakers is performed using a SVM with linear kernel trained following a LOSO-CV strategy per speech task. The results are reported in terms of the correct classification per class and of unweighted average recall (UA). The highest correct classification is obtained with the articulation model i.e., MFCC and GMM-UBM. The recognition rate of PD patients is 86.5% evaluating only the read sentences, while the highest UA is 81.9% when all of the tasks are combined. The highest recognition of speech recordings of PD patients (specificity) is 94.3%.

The imprecise articulation process, observed in PD speech, is studied by Rusz et al. in [Rusz 13]. The authors considered a group with 20 early PD patients and 15 HC, all of them were native Czech speakers. The authors analyzed vowel articulation across different speaking tasks including sustained phonations of the vowels /a/, /i/, and /u/, sentence repetition, read text, and monologue. The set of features comprises measures of F_1 and F_2, VAI, VSA, and the quotient F_{2i}/F_{2u}. The discrimination between PD and HC speakers was based on the minimax theorem [Schl 02]. The validation process was performed following the LOSO-CV strategy. The authors claim that sustained phonations are not appropriate to evaluate vowel articulation in PD patients, while monologue is the most sensitive task to differentiate between PD and HC. The results indicate that with articulation features it is possible to discriminate between PD and HC with classification scores of about 80%.

On the other hand, the impact of the LSVT® in the speech of patients with PD is analyzed with discriminative criterion by Tsanas et al. in [Tsan 14]. The authors measured a
total of 309 dysphonia features to assess whether a sustained phonation is "acceptable" or
"unacceptable" according to the clinical criteria of six experts. A total of 126 phonations
of the vowel /a/ uttered by 14 PD patients are evaluated i.e., each subject performed about
9 phonations. The LOGO (fit locally and think globally) feature selection algorithm is
applied to find the most discriminant subset of features [Sun 10]. Such subset is selected
following a 10-fold CV strategy. The feature selection process is repeated 100 times on the
training sets to avoid over-fitting. The final subset of features is formed following a voting
scheme. RF and SVM are used to discriminate between "acceptable" and "unacceptable"
phonations. The authors reported a classification score of 90% considering a subset of features with 10 measures. Although the methodology addressed in this study allows to do the
analysis with discriminative criterion, the CV strategy does not guarantee the speaker independence, since there is a high chance of including phonations of the same speaker into
the train and test subsets. Such validation process can lead to optimistic results and biased
conclusions. Also in 2014, Novotný et al., presented a study where different articulatory
deficits in speech of people with PD are modeled [Novo 14]. The authors considered a total
of 46 speakers, 24 of them with PD (20 male and 4 female). The group of HC includes
15 male and 7 female. All participants (PD and HC) had no history of speech therapy.
The speech task performed by the speakers consisted in the rapid repetition of the syllables
/pa-ta-ka/. The task was repeated twice per speaker. No limits in the number of repetitions
were imposed. The authors calculated 13 features to describe six different articulatory
aspects of speech including vowel quality, coordination of laryngeal and supralaryngeal
activity, precision of consonant articulation, tongue movement, occlusion weakening, and
speech timing. The classification procedure was performed by a SVM with Gaussian kernel. The complexity parameter C and the bandwidth of the kernel γ were chosen through
a grid-search such that $C \in [2^{-15}, 2^{-13}, ..., {}^{15}]$ and $\gamma \in [2^{-15}, 2^{-13}, ..., {}^{3}]$. The optimization
criterion was the highest accuracy obtained in the train subset, avoiding possible bias due
to over-fitting of the SVM. The authors reported a classification result of 88% in separating
speech signals of PD patients and HC. The results reported in this study confirm previous
observations made by another authors who reported imprecise articulation as the most predominant characteristic of PD-related dysarthria. These results suggest a step forward in
the automatic evaluation of articulation in PD speech, not only because it is made automatically, but also because the evaluation is performed with discriminative criterion, which
allows the analysis of accuracy, specificity, and sensitivity of the method. The drawback of
this study is that it was performed with a reduced number of participants, thus further experiments considering more patients are required in order to yield more conclusive results.

Further to the aforementioned characteristics in disordered speech, there are several
studies that document the manifestation of reduced stress in speech of people with motor
speech disorders [Wang 05, Pate 09]. However the mechanisms of stress production in PD
speech had not been thoroughly explored by objective methods. In [Tyka 14] the authors
analyzed stress patterns in five key words that were included in an equal number of sentences. A total of 36 male native Czech speakers were recorded, 20 of them with PD.
Semi-automatic acoustic analyses were performed using Praat [Boer 01] and consisted in
pitch, intensity, and duration measurements. The measures were corrected manually by an
expert when necessary. Additionally, the authors introduced the stress pattern index (SPI)

which is defined as $\text{SPI} = (1 - \ln(\frac{F0_{max}}{F0_{min}})) \sum E_n$, where $\sum E_n$ is the cumulative sum of signal energy. The effect of the inter-subject variability in the F_0 estimates is minimized by using the logarithmic expression of F_0. The SPI is designed to mirror the acoustic effect of exaggerated pitch, intensity, and duration. According to the results, it seems like PD patients have a reduced ability to produce contrastive stress in particular key words. Further research is required to obtain more conclusive results.

The most recent studies considering PD speech have been focused not only on the automatic discrimination of PD and HC speakers, but also on the evaluation of the neurological state of the patient and/or the effect of dopaminergic treatment in Parkinsonian speech. In [Baye 15] Bayestehtashk et al. performed the automatic evaluation of the neurological state of PD patients through speech. The authors considered a group of 168 patients. The speech tasks evaluated during the study include, (1) sustained phonations of the English vowel /a/, (2) DDK evaluation, and (3) read text. A total of 1582 measures are calculated using the openSMILE toolkit [Eybe 10]. The patients were labeled by neurologists experts according to the UPDRS motor scale. The accuracy of the model is tested using three different regression techniques to evaluate the severity of the disease. The authors report that the error obtained with ridge regression is lower than those obtained with lasso and support vector regression. The features extracted from the read texts are the most effective and robust to quantify the extent of the disease. The mean absolute error obtained with respect to the motor section of the UPDRS scale is about 5.5, with a baseline of 8.0. The strategy to optimize the parameters of the model, to measure the performance of the system, and to validate the model was LOSO-CV. The authors conclude that considerable work is still required to improve the accuracy of inference. Additionally, they claim that the perceptual characteristics in PD speech such as imprecise articulation, short rushes of speech, and language impairments are still not modeled in the literature of PD. They also stated that further work is required to present the information to the clinicians in a useful and interpretable manner. The effect of dopaminergic treatment in the speech of PD patients is studied by Tykalová et al. in [Tyka 15]. A total of 14 PD patients and 14 age- and gender-matched HC were recruited for this study. The subjects were examined three times, one before starting the dopaminergic medication, and twice within the next 6 years. The authors calculated the percentage of dysfluent words pronounced in a monologue and a red text. Additionally, the articulation accuracy was calculated as the F_{2i}/F_{2u} ratio measured following the methodology presented in [Rusz 13]. According to the results, the speech of PD patients is more dysfluent after 3-6 years of dopaminergic therapy than the speech of HC. This finding indicate that there is an adverse effect of the prolonged dopaminergic therapy in the fluency of PD speech. This study shows an interesting evidence with important implications in clinical practice. However, considering the low number of evaluated patients, further research is required to gather more conclusive results. Also, since the longitudinal studies can be influenced by different acoustic conditions, it must be managed with special attention.

As it is shown in the reviewed literature, the analysis of speech of people with PD has evolved in both, Medical and Engineering fields. This evolution, in terms of number of contributions, is shown in Figure 1.1.

Table 1.1 summarizes the reviewed literature. The sub-systems of speech that are studied on each contribution are indicated with 'X'. Note that there is only one contribution considering resonance in speech. Although it is already known that hypernasality is not sa-

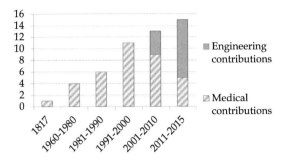

Figure 1.1: Summary of the contributions reviewed in the state-of-the-art.

lient in Parkinsonian speech, this revision of literature shows that could be worth to address further research on this phenomenon.

According to the reviewed literature, the main aspects considered for modeling dysarthric speech signals in people with Parkinson's disease can be summarized in the following items.

- The phonation dimension of speech has been widely covered and analyzed considering different sets of features including stability, periodicity, noise content, nonlinear structure, spectral wealth, and others.

- Articulation has also been addressed in different papers. However, most of them are focused on vowel articulation. Thus, considering that PD patients develop problems to pronounce stop and voiceless consonants correctly [Gobe 08], further research is required to model consonant sounds, unvoiced frames, and other speech units that require the control of muscles and limbs involved in the articulation process.

- Prosodic characteristics provide information about speech rate, pause, intonation, and general communication skills of people. These characteristics must be included in the evaluation of PD speech for a better understanding of the impact of the disease in speech [Skod 08].

- Notwithstanding the evidence reported by clinicians, the research community has been mainly focused in modeling voiced frames. The scientists have modeled the vocal folds movements accurately; however, as it is highlighted in several works [Loge 81], [Duff 00], and [Gobe 08], for the case of dysarthric speech, there is also important information in the frames where the vocal folds should not vibrate i.e., pauses and unvoiced frames. The modeling of the loss of motor control to produce unvoiced frames should improve the modeling of speech of people with PD.

- Although there are evidence supporting the convenience of studying consonant sounds produced by PD patients [Wals 11]. The existing studies have addressed this phenomenon from the temporal point of view but there are no studies addressing such

Table 1.1: Summary of contributions in Medical and Engineering fields.

Paper	Brief description of the data	Phon.	Art.	Pros.	Lang.
[Loge 81]	200 PD. Consonants.	X	X		Eng
[Robb 86]	6 PD, 6 HC.	X	X		Eng
[Forr 89]	9 PD, 8 HC. Read texts.	X	X		Eng
[Acke 91]	12 PD, 12 HC.	X	X		Eng
[Pere 96]	22 PD	X			Spa
[Gamb 97]	41 PD. Sustained vowel and read texts.	X			Spa
[Le D 98]	10 PD, 20 HC. Read texts.			X	Eng
[Jack 99]	24 PD, 17 HC. Sustained vowel.	X			Eng
[Benk 00]	53 PD. Spontaneous speech, read texts, and isolated words.		X		Eng
[Rami 01]	33 PD. LSVT and RET programs.	X			Eng
[Gobe 05]	12 PD. Read texts and monologue.		X	X	Eng
[Skod 08]	121 PD, 70 HC. Read texts.		X	X	Ger
[Wats 08]	10 PD, 10 HC. Isolated words.		X		Eng
[Gobe 08]	9 PD, 8 HC. Read texts.	X		X	Eng
[Sapi 10]	38 PD, 14 HC. Read texts.		X		Eng
[Skod 10]	73 PD, 43 HC. DDK evaluation.		X	X	Ger
[Wals 11]	16 PD, 16 HC. Read texts.		X		Eng
[Skod 11a]	169 PD, 64 HC. Read texts.		X	X	Ger
[Skod 11c]	68 PD, 32 HC. Read texts.		X	X	Ger
[Skod 12]	67 PD, 40 HC. Read text.		X	X	Ger
[Flas 12]	60 PD. Read texts and DDK evaluation		X	X	Eng
[Skod 13]	80 PD, 60 HC. Read texts.	X	X	X	Ger
[Litt 09]	23 PD, 8 HC. Sustained vowel.	X			Eng
[Saka 10]	23 PD, 8 HC. Sustained vowel.	X			Eng
[Tsan 10b]	42 PD. Sustained vowel.	X			Eng
[Tsan 11]	42 PD. Sustained vowel.	X			Eng
[Rusz 11]	23 PD, 23 HC. Sustained vowel, read texts, DDK evaluation.	X	X	X	Czh
[Tsan 12]	43 PD. Sustained vowel.	X			Eng
[Bock 13]	88 PD, 88 HC. Sustained vowel, read texts, DDK evaluation, monologue.	X	X	X	Ger
[Rusz 13]	20 PC, 15 HC. Sustained vowel, read texts, monologue.		X		Czh
[Tsan 14]	14 PD. Sustained vowel.	X			Eng
[Novo 14]	24 PD, 22 HC. DDK evaluation.		X		Czh
[Tyka 14]	20 PD, 16 HC. Read sentences.		X	X	Czh
[Baye 15]	168 PD. Sustained vowel, read texts, DDK evaluation.	X	X	X	Eng
[Tyka 15]	14 PD, 14 HC. Read texts, monologue.		X		Czh

Phon: Phonation. Art: Articulation. Pros: Prosody. Lang: Language.
Eng: English. Spa: Spanish. Ger: German. Czh: Czech

phenomenon considering the energy content of the speech segments during the production of consonants and/or during the transition between voiced and unvoiced sounds.

- There are no studies evaluating the reliability of characterization and classification methods to discriminate between PD and HC speakers considering speech recordings in different languages.

- One of the aims of the research community in speech processing is to provide the patients and clinicians with technology able to objectively evaluate speech impairments of people with PD. Computational tools to guide and assess the speech therapy of the patients are also in the scope of the research community. However, the development of those technologies and computational tools must take into account that realistic scenarios will include speech signals recorded in non-controlled acoustic conditions.

1.3. Contributions to the research on the analysis of speech of people with Parkinson's disease

The overview of research on speech impairments due to Parkinson's disease shows that several aspects of speech have been analyzed and different classification and regression techniques have been tested. It indicates that there is still a great interest of the research community to understand and model different phenomena in speech of people with PD. In order to contribute to this aim, the following are the main outcomes of this thesis.

- The PC-GITA database has been built to make possible the analysis of several phenomena in speech of native Spanish speaking PD patients. This database contains recordings of 50 PD and 50 gender- and age-matched HC speakers. All of them were recorded in the sound-proof booth that was built during a research project funded by ARTICA [Oroz 11]. The database provides speech recordings of several tasks including sustained vowels, isolated words, isolated sentences, read texts, and monologues. This database was used to organize one of the special sessions of the 15th Annual Conference of the International Speech Communication Association (INTERSPEECH)[4] in 2015. The details of the data collection process and the included speech tasks can be found in Chapter 3.

- The energy content in unvoiced frames and in the transitions between voiced and unvoiced sounds in speech is proposed as a new modeling approach to discriminate between PD and HC speakers with high classification accuracies.

- The modeling approach proposed in this thesis has been tested in databases with recordings in Spanish, German, and Czech languages, obtaining high accuracies in all of the tests. According to the reviewed literature, this is the first study in analysis of Parkinson's speech that considers recordings of three different languages. The experiments addressed in this thesis indicate that it is possible to design computational

---

[4]`http://emotion-research.net/sigs/speech-sig/is15-compare`
Last retrieved 7/2/2015.

systems to assess the speech of PD patients in different languages, enabling the easy and fast deployment of this technology in several countries.

- The characterization method introduced in this thesis is tested with speech signals recorded in non-controlled noise conditions and shows to be also robust in such scenarios.

- Features from the three different speech dimensions i.e., phonation, articulation, and prosody, are used to predict the neurological state of the PD patients included in PC-GITA. According to the results, the phonation and articulation measures are the most suitable to perform the prediction.

1.4. Structure of this work

Chapter 2 describes different phenomena that are present in the speech of people with PD. The existing tools and methods for the evaluation of Parkinson's speech are also described.

Chapter 3 provides the details of PC-GITA, including the technical description of the tools used during the recording sessions and the speech tasks included in the evaluations. Details of the German and Czech data considered in the experiments of the thesis are also included.

Chapter 4 describes the features that are considered in this thesis to model the speech signals. Those features are grouped considering three dimensions of speech: phonation, articulation, and prosody. The chapter includes also details of the mathematical methods that are used in this work to perform the automatic discrimination of people with PD and healthy speakers, and also to estimate the neurological state of the patients.

Chapter 5 includes the details of the experiments that are addressed to evaluate the capability of the reviewed features to discriminate between PD and HC speakers. The regression experiments to predict the neurological state of the patients are also presented. At the end of this chapter there is an extensive discussion about the performed experiments and their results.

Chapter 6 includes a brief summary of the lessons learned during the collection of the PC-GITA recordings and presents an outlook on future research in the area of Parkinson's speech analysis.

Chapter 7 summarizes the analyzed aspects of Parkinson's speech signals and the main experimental results.

Chapter 2

Speech of people with Parkinson's disease

2.1. Why does Parkinson's disease affect speech?

To explain why speech is affected by PD, it is necessary to introduce basic knowledge of the brain anatomy regarding the motor control and planning for speech production. This thesis does not pretends to replace a course of Neurology and the information enclosed here is only with the propose of giving a general idea to the reader of how the speech production process is affected by Parkinson's disease.

The cortex of the brain is composed by several parts, two of them are in charged of the motor execution and planning i.e., motor and pre-motor cortex, respectively. Part of the area that is involved in the control of speech belongs also to the motor and pre-motor cortex. Figure 2.1[1] illustrates these basic parts of the brain.

Most of the internal brain areas involved in motor activities can be studied taking a coronal section of the brain, in the basal ganglia. Figure 2.2[2] illustrates such section and includes some of the parts involved in motor activities. The movement of muscles is planned in the pre-motor cortex, which projects the "order" to the Striatum (formed by Caudate and Putamen). The Striatum projects to the Globus Pallidus (GP), which contains output neurons of the Basal Ganglia and in turn projects to the ventral anterior and lateral nucleus (VA-VL) in the motor Thalamus in order to give the "order" to the motor cortex, which finally sends the "information" to the corresponding muscles to execute the movement.

For a better understanding of how the brain smoothly orchestrates motor behaviors, it is necessary to study the basal ganglia circuit, which affects the movements in the contralateral body i.e., the circuit in the left-side of the brain controls movements of the muscles in

---

[1]This figure is an adapted version of the picture shared in
http://commons.wikimedia.org/wiki/File:Precentral_gyrus_3d.png
Last retrieved 7/2/2015, under the Creative Commons Attribution-Share Alike 2.1 Japan license.
[2]This figure is an adapted version of the picture shared in
http://commons.wikimedia.org/wiki/File:Basal-ganglia-coronal-sections-large.png
Last retrieved 7/2/2015, under the Creative Commons Attribution-Share Alike 3.0 Unported license.

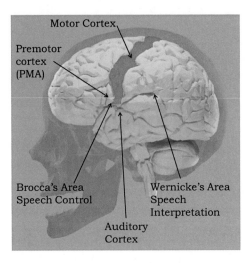

Figure 2.1: Cortical areas involved in motor planning and execution.

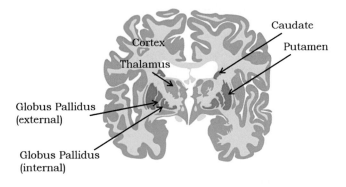

Figure 2.2: Coronal section of the brain: basal ganglia.

the right-side of the body and vice versa. An schematic picture of the process is illustrated in Figure 2.3 [3].

There are two ways to excite neurons in the motor thalamus, direct and indirect pathways. The main difference is the inhibition of neurons in the subthalamic nucleus before exciting the Globus Pallidus internal (GP_i), which occurs in the indirect pathway, but not in the direct one.

---

[3]This figure is an adapted version of a picture in http://www.brainhq.com/
Last retrieved 7/2/2015.
It is used with explicit permission of the original authors.

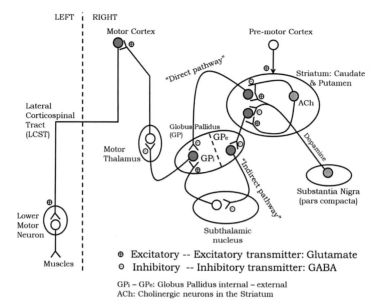

Figure 2.3: Basal ganglia circuit.

The direct pathway: Fibers in the pre-motor cortex excite the neurons in the Striatum (Caudate & Putamen) through Glutamate neurotransmitters. Those cells inhibit the neurons in the GP$_i$ through Gamma-aminobutyric acid (GABA) neurotransmitters. More inhibition in the GP$_i$ means less inhibition in the motor thalamus, which in turn results in more firing of the neurons in the motor cortex, thus increasing the thalamic input to the motor cortex i.e., the direct pathway turns up the motor activity.

The indirect pathway: In this case the neurons in the Striatum that are excited by the pre-motor cortex inhibit the cells in the GP$_e$ which in turn inhibit the neurons of the subthalamic nucleus, thus subthalamic cells are dis-inhibited and increase their activity, resulting in more excitation to the GP$_i$ neurons. GP$_i$ increases their inhibition in the motor thalamus, which is reflected in turning down the motor activity in the motor cortex.

Dopaminergic and cholinergic neurons in motor control: Dopamine is produced by cells in the pars compacta of the substantia nigra (SNc). Dopaminergic neurons release dopamine into the Striatum and their effect is excitatory upon cells involved in the direct pathway and inhibitory upon cells in the indirect pathway. On the other hand, cholinergic (also called Acetylcholine – ACh) neurons inhibit the striatal cells of the direct pathway and excite cells in the indirect pathway.

Effect of Parkinson's disease: PD is characterized by the loss of dopaminergic neurons in the SNc. As the direct pathway turns up the motor activity, and dopamine has an excitatory role upon the striatal neurons, the motor activity of a person suffering from PD will goes down due to a double adverse effect in the direct pathway, i.e., loss of excitation from dopamine and the ongoing inhibitory effect of ACh neurons. The end result is more inhibition reaching the motor thalamus, which makes the motor cortex less active. This symptom is known as *hypokinesia* and it is the hallmark of Parkinson's disease. Such symptom affects the motor control of all muscles in the body, including those involved in the production of speech. That is the reason of using the term *hypokinetic dysarthria* to enclose most of the symptoms observed in the speech of people with PD. A similar analysis can be made on the indirect pathway. The dopamine inhibits the indirect pathway. When PD takes away such inhibition, there is an increment of the indirect pathway activity. At the same time there is an excitatory effect of the ACh neurons upon the indirect pathway, turning down the motor activity.

Dopaminergic treatment: PD patients have decreased levels of dopaminergic neurons in the Striatum and SNc. They can be treated with dopaminergic drugs such as L-dopa in order to compensate the loss of dopaminergic neurons. Parkinson's patients can also be treated with drugs that decrease the level of ACh neurons in the Striatum. Both treatments increase the activity of the direct pathway and decrease the activity in the indirect pathway (see Figure 2.3).

2.2.   Characteristics of PD speech

The loss of control in the motor activity leads PD patients to develop different voice and speech impairments including reduced loudness, monopitch, monoloudness, reduced stress, breathy, hoarse voice quality, and imprecise articulation [Rami 08]. These impairments are called *hypokinetic dysarthria* [Loge 78]. The dysarthric speech is characterized for several abnormal patterns in the subsystems of speech i.e., phonation, articulation, and prosody. Phonation is defined as the vibration of vocal folds to produce sounds, articulation comprises the modification of the position, stress, and shape of organs and tissues involved in speech production, and prosody is the variation of loudness, pitch, and timing to produce natural speech [Gobe 05]. From the clinical point of view, phonation problems are related to vocal fold bowing and incomplete closing of vocal folds [Pere 96]. Articulation deficits are manifested as reduced amplitude and velocity of the articulatory movements of lips, jaw, and tongue [Skod 11c], and prosody impairments are manifested as monopitch, monoloudness and changes in speech rate and pauses [Rusz 11], and difficulties to express emotions through speech [Mobe 08].

In [Crit 81] the author observed the following effect of the disease in the patients:

> "The initial defect in the untreated patient is a failure to control respiration to produce speech, and there follows a forward progression of articulatory symptoms involving larynx, pharynx, tongue, and finally lips".

Disorders in postural fixation of the tongue with disorders in articulation rate and palatal paralysis are also observed. Regarding the impairments in prosody e.g., speech rate, Critchley reports that inappropriate silences, short rushes of speech, and rate variation can also be observed in PD patients [Crit 81]. The abnormal rate of speech suggests, a desire of the patient to complete the sentence during a single breath. Similarly, there is an extra-effort in the initiation of speech to release the rigidity of articulatory and phonatory musculature.

Further to the aforementioned speech impairments observed in PD patients, Benke et al. reported several repetitive speech phenomena [Benk 00]. The repetitions of speech were observed in two variants, one is hyperfluent which formally is known as palilalia [Acke 89], and the other is dysfluent, which can be described as stuttering-like speech.

Duffy [Duff 00] defines dysarthria as a "neuromuscular disturbance of strength, speed, tone, steadiness, or accuracy of the movements that underlie the execution of speech". According to his observations, the pathophysiology of PD has effects that may be evident in the respiratory, laryngeal, velopharyngeal, and articulatory components of speech production. Considering the negative effect of the disease in the function of the motor cortex, Parkinson's patients can also develop impaired control of the vagus and hypoglossal nerves, inducing problems to pronounce consonants that require pressure build-up in the mouth and lingual movements, respectively [Duff 00]. The most serious pronunciation problems occur mainly in the plosive consonants /p/, /t/, /k/, /b/, /d/, and /g/, which appear as a result of the developed impairments to control nerves and muscles involved in the movement of different articulatory organs, such as lips, tongue tip, center of the tongue, tongue base, jaw, epiglottis, and larynx [Loge 81].

2.3. Existing scales to assess PD patients

There exist several scales to assess the neurological state of PD patients. The most widely used are the Unified Parkinson's Disease Rating Scale (UPDRS) and the Hoehn & Yahr scale. Both are described in the following subsections.

2.3.1. Unified Parkinson's Disease Rating Scale (UPDRS)

There are different versions of this scale, the most updated one is called MDS-UPDRS (Movement Disorders Society sponsored revision of the Parkinson's Disease Rating Scale) [Goet 08]. This version assesses motor and non-motor aspects of PD. It has four parts, part I evaluates non-motor experiences of daily living (13 items), part II comprises motor experiences of daily living (13 items), part III includes the motor examination (33 items), and part IV is to assess the motor complications (6 items) [4].
The ratings of each item range from 0 (normal) to 4 (severe) and the total score for each part is obtained from the sum of the corresponding items. The impact of PD in speech is considered only in one item; however, as the motor sub-scale (part III) reflects motor problems, it is typically used as the ground truth to label the patients in different experiments of pattern recognition. In this case the speech recordings of each patient are labeled with scores ranging between 0 and 132 (33 items $\times$ 4 = 132).

The MDS-UPRDS scale is specifically designed to assess PD patients and its reliability was validated with satisfactory results via test-retest trial performed with 435 patients from five countries. Although the scale has several strengths like its wide utilization across

---

[4]Further details of the MDS-UPDRS scale can be found in
http://www.movementdisorders.org/publications/rating_scales/
Last retrieved 7/2/2015

the clinical spectrum of PD, its coverage of motor and non-motor symptoms, and its clinimetric properties (reliability and validity) [Mart 14], the evaluation of speech represents just one item and typically the neurologist is not trained to assess/screen different speech impairments suffered by the patients.

The previous version of the scale is simply called UPDRS. It assesses PD-related disability and impairment. It is composed by 42 items, 4 about mentation, behavior, and mood, 13 items about activities of daily living, 27 items about motor activities, and 11 items about complications of therapy. This version of the scale was reviewed by Movement Disorder Society Task Force on Rating Scales for Parkinson's disease [Move 03]. The authors highlighted its wide utilization and application in PD; however, its weaknesses include the absence of screening questions on several important non-motor aspects. In the paper, the Task Force recommended the Movement Disorder Society to sponsor de development of the MDS-UPDRS scale.

2.3.2. Hoehn & Yahr scale (H&Y)

This scale was designed originally to provide a general estimate of clinical function in PD, combining functional deficits and objective signs. The scale comprises a set of five stages where 1 is associated to a minimal or no functional disability and 5 is assigned to patients who are confined in bed or wheelchair unless aided. There are two variants of the scale, the original one with integer values for the stages from 1 to 5, and the modified one which ranges also between 1 to 5 but with increments of 0.5.

H&Y scale is widely used, even there is one item in the MDS-UPDRS scale (not counted in the total value) that corresponds to the H&Y state. According to the Movement Disorder Society [Goet 04] higher stages labeled with this scale correlate with neuroimaging studies of dopaminergic loss and also exhibit high correlations with other standardized motor scales. Although its wide use and acceptance, H&Y scale has several weaknesses, such as the non inclusion of non-motor problems, its non-linearity, the mixture of impairments and disabilities, and its high weight towards postural instability, excluding impairments or disabilities from other motor symptoms. This scale does not consider the explicit evaluation of speech impairments in the patients, however, there are several studies in speech analysis which take this scale as baseline to perform regression tasks, multi-class classification, or statistical analysis.

2.4. Existing methods and tools for speech therapy in PD patients

There are different medical therapies and surgery procedures such as deep brain stimulation that have shown significant improvements in motor functions of patients with PD [Wort 13]; however, their impact on speech production remains unclear [Rami 08, Skod 11b]. Considering that there is a lack of methods and therapies for PD patients to improve their oral communication skills, several researchers have designed strategies and in some cases devices to contribute in delaying the impact of PD in speech.

2.4.1.   Lee Silverman Voice Test (LSVT)

In 1987 the LSVT was proposed as an auto-therapy guide (protocol) to improve the speech of PD patients [King 94, Rami 94, Rami 88]. The protocol includes five tasks: pronunciation of the vowel /a/ in a sustained manner, sustained phonation of the vowel /a/ while the patient is decreasing the tone, sustained phonation of the vowel /a/ while the patient is increasing the tone, reading of ten isolated words, and finally reading of a text with 10 words[5]. The LSVT is applied worldwide and has demonstrated its effectiveness after 6 months of constant speech therapy [Sapi 07]. However, it does not includes the objective evaluation of the voice signals and it was not designed with the aim of analyzing specific aspects in the speech which are related to the communication process such as articulation, prosody, and intelligibility.

2.4.2.   Pitch Limiting Voice Treatment (PLVT)

The set of speech exercises proposed in the PLVT treatment is presented in [Bang 03]. It includes exercises to improve the posture and relaxation and ask the patient to speak loudly and low. The aim is to reduce stress in the jaw and larynx. Prosody exercises are also included asking the patient to pronounce, syllable by syllable, each word of a text. The general aim of the therapy is to make the patients to be able to talk loud and low in different situations during their daily life.

In [de S 03] de Swart et al. presented a paper comparing LSVT and PLVT. According to their observations, PLVT has proved to be successful in practice and it is as easy and effective as LSVT. The main difference between LSVT and PLVT is that the first raises the pitch in all tasks, whereas the second prevents a rise in pitch in all tasks except for an exercise that consists in reciting. Both therapies result in an immediate significant improvement in loudness. According to de Swart et al., the advantages of PLVT are in the fact that speaking with a low voice prevents a rise in laryngeal muscle tone, resulting in a lower laryngeal resistance and less rigid vocal cords.

2.4.3.   Computational tools for the assessment and guidance of speech therapy

Several studies have been focused on the development of portable devices to assess different speech disorders. In [Zick 80] the authors present a portable device to assess the speech therapy of patients with PD. The device provides bio-feedback according to the speech volume levels. A sound tone is sent to the patient if the vocal intensity falls below an adjustable threshold. This device operates with a microphone stuck to the neck of the patients, which could be considered invasive in some way by several users. This device was updated later in [Rubo 85], where the authors included visual-feedback. However, the new version still requires the microphone stuck to the neck. In [Goet 09] the authors present a computer based at-home testing device (AHTD). This tool is developed to assess several symptoms of PD patients such as tremor, small and large bradykinesia, speech, reaction/movement times, among others. According to their findings, the incorporation of

---

[5]www.lsvtglobal.com
Last retrieved 7/2/2015.

the AHTD in larger clinical studies is feasible and it could be used to follow the progress of the disease. In [Vire 11] the authors developed a device equipped with an accelerometer to measure the skin vibrations and a microphone to record the speech signal. The device calculates three voice parameters: the fundamental frequency, the energy content, and the sound pressure level. The feedback is given via vibrations i.e., the device vibrates to inform the patient that is speaking incorrectly. In [Caru 13] the authors present a portable device to record speech signals from patients under monitoring. The signals are captured using a microphone stuck to the neck of the patient. The aim of this device is to identify different voice disorders by the estimation of the fundamental frequency and the sound pressure level.

Although there are several studies focused on developing computational tools to assess the speech of PD patients, there is a lack of prototypes or products that give accurate and interpretable information to the patient and the medical expert. The specific evaluation of different aspects in speech such as articulation, prosody, and intelligibility have not included so far. However, the current signal processing and pattern recognition techniques make possible to think on the development of devices to assess these aspects in speech and even to assess specific motor activity of different articulators e.g., tongue, lips, jaw, and velum. These kind of devices or platforms could help the experts to guide their decisions regarding the therapy of the patients and telemonitoring could be also included through an Internet connection.

Summary: The state-of-the-art and the impact of PD in speech have been reviewed in these two chapters. Chapter 1 comprises an overview of techniques used to model PD speech and shows how those techniques have contributed in clinical and medical studies. Chapter 2 includes general concepts of neuroanatomy with the aim of illustrate why PD affects speech and which are the implications of such impairments. These two chapters show that it is worth to study the speech of people with PD considering three dimensions: phonation, articulation, and prosody. These dimensions can reflect several motor aspects of speech such as the process to control the vibration of the vocal folds, the control of different articulators to produce consonant sounds, and the control of intonation and timing to produce intelligible speech signals. In order to study all these phenomena, this thesis considers sustained phonation of vowels, continuous speech signals, and also the rapid repetition of syllables which is a specific task that allow the analysis of particular movements performed while the patient is speaking. The methodology proposed in this thesis is applied upon three databases with recordings of three different languages: Spanish, German, and Czech. Details of the recordings considered in each database are included in the next chapter.

Chapter 3

Data collection

This chapter includes the details of the process followed to build the Parkinson's Condition – GITA (PC-GITA) database. The name comes from the research group GITA (*Grupo de Investigación en Telecomunicaciones Aplicadas*) from Universidad de Antioquia. The description of the data from native German and Czech speakers is also included in this chapter. As I did not participate in the collection of such data, the details of this process are not provided. The use of speech data with recordings of different languages and captured in different acoustic conditions, requires the application and design of methods that are independent of the spoken language. Additionally, the robustness and generalization capability of the methods can be analyzed.

3.1. Spanish

From the literature reviewed in Chapter 1, it is possible to observe that one of the main issues that might be addressed by people working on pathological speech analysis is the construction of databases, following a well designed recording protocol, and including recordings with different speech tasks. The construction of a speech database is particularly difficult if we consider the shortage of people willing to participate in research programs and, in the specific case of PD patients, their mobility limitations.

3.1.1. Recruitment process

More than 100 speakers were recruited for this study; however, only 50 PD patients and 50 HC were included in the final version of the database. Some PD speakers were excluded because they were not diagnosed with PD or because additional speech impairments different to those associated to PD were observed by the phoniatry expert during the speech evaluation. The inclusion criteria for the HC group were their healthy condition and the age and gender matching with respect to the PD patients. Most of the recorded patients participate in the weekly meetings of *Fundalianza Parkinson Colombia*[1]. The recording sessions were performed at Clínica Noel, in Medellín, Colombia[2]. Due their mobility difficulties, was necessary to fetch the patients from their houses to the Clinic

---

[1]http://www.fundalianzaparkinson.org/
[2]http://www.clinicanoel.org.co/
Last retrieved 7/2/2015.

and bring them back to their houses after the evaluation. Similarly, as the healthy people do not feel the necessity to visit a doctor, was necessary to fetch most of them from their houses.

3.1.2. General description of the participants and technical conditions for the recording process

The database includes speech recordings of 50 people with PD and 50 healthy controls, 25 male and 25 female on each group. All the participants are native Colombian Spanish speakers. The age of the male with PD ranges from 33 to 81 years old (mean 61.6 ± 11.2), the age of the female with PD ranges from 49 to 75 years old (mean 60.7 ± 7.3). For the case of healthy controls, the age of the male ranges from 31 to 86 (mean 60.3 ± 11.6) and the age of the female ranges from 49 to 76 years old (mean 61.4 ± 7.0). Therefore, the database is well balanced in terms of age and gender. The recordings were captured in noise controlled conditions, in the sound proof booth that was built at the Clínica Noel, in Medellín, Colombia [Oroz 11]. The voice registers were sampled at 44100 Hz with 16-bit resolution, using a dynamic omnidirectional microphone (Shure, SM 63L) which is commonly used for professional applications. The recordings were captured using a professional audio card with up to 24 bits and such that supports up to 96 Kbps of sampling rates (M-Audio, Fast Track C400). All of the patients were diagnosed by a neurologist expert and were labeled according to the MDS-UPDRS and the modified H&Y scales; the recording of the speech samples were done with the patients in ON-state, i.e., no more than 3 hours after the morning medication. None of the healthy control had symptoms associated to PD or any other neurological disease. The recording procedure is in compliance with the Helsinki Declaration and was approved by the Ethics Committee of the Clínica Noel, in Medellín, Colombia, and a written informed consent was signed by each participant.

Details of age, MDS-UPDRS-III, and H&Y values, along with time post PD diagnosis of the PD patients are included in Table 3.1. The table is divided in the middle by a double line, the left side includes data from the male participants and the right side indicates the data of the female speakers. The fifth and tenth columns show the age of the male and female healthy participants, respectively.

The distributions of the age, MDS-UPDRS III (motor section), and the time post the diagnosis of the disease are illustrated in Figure 3.1.

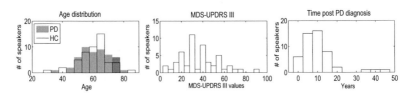

Figure 3.1: Spanish – Distribution of age, MDS-UPDRS III values, and time post PD diagnosis.

M - PD				M - HC	F - PD				F - HC
Age	UPDRS	H&Y	t	Age	Age	UPDRS	H&Y	t	AGE
81	5	2	12	86	75	52	3	3	75
77	92	5	15	76	73	38	2	4	73
75	13	1	1	71	72	19	2	2.5	76
75	75	3	16	68	70	23	2	12	68
74	40	2.5	12	68	69	19	2	12	65
69	40	3	5	67	66	28	2	4	65
68	14	1	1	67	66	28	2	4	64
68	67	4	20	67	65	54	3	8	63
68	65	3	8	67	64	40	2	3	63
67	28	2	4	65	62	42	3	12	63
65	32	2	12	64	61	21	1	4	63
65	53	2	19	63	60	29	2	7	62
64	28	2	3	63	59	40	2	14	62
64	45	2	3	62	59	71	3	17	61
60	44	3	10	60	58	57	2	1	61
59	6	1	8	59	57	41	3	37	61
57	20	2	0.4	56	57	61	3	17	60
56	30	2	14	55	55	30	2	12	58
54	15	3	4	55	55	43	3	12	57
50	53	2	7	54	55	30	2	12	57
50	19	2	17	51	55	29	2	43	55
48	9	3	12	50	54	30	2	7	55
47	33	2	2	42	51	38	3	41	50
45	21	1	7	42	51	23	2	10	50
33	51	2	9	31	49	53	2	16	49

M - PD: Male - Parkinson's Disease, **M - HC**: Male - Healthy Control
F - PD: Female - Parkinson's Disease, **F - HC**: Female - Healthy Control
t: time post PD diagnosis (in years).

Table 3.1: Clinical information of the PD patients and age of the healthy speakers.

3.1.3. Speech tasks

The recording protocol considers different tasks which were designed to analyze several aspects of the voice and speech of people with PD including phonation, articulation, prosody, and intelligibility.

Sustained phonations

1. Three repetitions of the five Spanish vowels uttered in a sustained manner.

2. The five Spanish vowels uttered changing the tone of each vowel from low to high.

Diadochokinetic evaluation and isolated words

1. Rapid repetition of the following words and phonemes (diadochokinetic evaluation): /pa-ta-ka/, /pa-ka-ta/, /pe-ta-ka/, /pa/, /ta/, /ka/.

2. Repetition of a set with different isolated words grouped into three subsets:

   Set 1 - Words that form a phonological inventory of the Colombian Spanish: petaca, bodega, pato, apto, campana, presa, plato, braso[3], blusa, trato, atleta, drama, grito, globo, crema, clavo, fruta, flecha, viaje, llueve, caucho, reina, ñame, coco, gato.

   Set 2 - Motor verbs: acariciar, aplaudir, agarrar, dibujar, patalear, pisotear, trotar, sonreír, soplar, masticar.

   Set 3 - Nouns naming concrete objects: barco, bosque, ciudad, establo, hospital, luna, montaña, nube, puente, tractor.

Isolated sentences, read text, and spontaneous speech

1. Repetition of six different complex and simple sentences (from the syntactic point of view):

   a) Mi casa tiene tres cuartos. (Simple)

   b) Omar, que vive cerca, trajo miel. (Complex)

   c) Laura sube al tren que pasa. (Complex)

   d) Los libros nuevos no caben en la mesa de la oficina. (Simple)

   e) Rosita Niño, que pinta bien, donó sus cuadros ayer. (Complex)

   f) Luisa Rey compra el colchón duro que tanto le gusta. (Complex)

2. Reading of a dialog between a doctor (**D**) and a patient (**P**). This text has 36 words and it is phonetically balanced. It contains most of the Spanish sounds (spoken in Colombia). The dialog is as follows:

   P: Ayer fui al médico.
   D: Qué le pasa? Me preguntó.

---

[3]Although the correct writing of this word is with 'z', it is written here with 's' to indicate the sound in the Colombian Spanish which is like an 's', but not like the Spanish 'z'.

P: Yo le dije: Ay doctor! Donde pongo el dedo me duele.
D: Tiene la uña rota?
P: Sí.
D: Pues ya sabemos qué es. Deje su cheque a la salida.

3. Reading of sentences with additional emphasis in particular words (marked with capital letters). The sentences are detailed below:

   a) Viste las noticias? Yo vi GANAR la medalla de plata en pesas. Ese muchacho tiene mucha fuerza!

   b) Juan se ROMPIÓ una PIERNA cuando iba en la MOTO.

   c) Estoy muy triste, ayer vi MORIR a un amigo.

   d) Estoy muy preocupado, cada vez me es más difícil HABLAR.

4. Spontaneous speech: it is a monologue where the participants were asked to speak about what they commonly do in a normal day i.e., at what time they wake up, what kind of activities they do during the morning and in the afternoon, etc. The average duration of the monologues is 48 ± 29 seconds and 45 ± 24 seconds for PD and HC groups, respectively.

The original document with the protocol and the informed consent that was designed to perform the speech recordings is provided in the Appendix A. This evaluation protocol takes between eight to ten minutes to be administered which allows the phoniatry experts to perform other kind of specific screenings or exercises that they do during a normal clinical evaluation.

This dataset was used to organize one of the sub-challenges of the INTERSPEECH 2015 Computational Paralinguistics Challenge (ComParE)[4].

3.2. German

This corpus consists of 176 native German speakers. The set of patients includes 88 speakers (47 male and 41 female). The age of male patients ranges between 44 and 82 (mean 66.7 ± 8.4), and the age of the female patients ranges from 42 to 84 (mean 66.2 ± 9.7). The HC group contains 88 speakers (44 male, 44 female). The age of male participants ranges from 26 to 83 (mean 63.8 ± 12.7), and the age of the female is between 54 to 79 (mean 62.6 ± 15.2). The patients were evaluated by neurologist experts according to the UPDRS-III (motor section of the UPDRS) and Hoehn & Yahr scales and the mean values are 22.7 ± 10.9 and 2.4 ± 0.6, respectively. The average duration of the disease prior to the recording session is 7.1 ± 5.8 years. The speech samples were recorded with the patients in ON-state. The voice signals were sampled at 16 kHz with 16-bit resolution.

The distributions of the age, UPDRS-III, and the time post the diagnosis of the disease are illustrated in Figure 3.2.

---

[4]`http://emotion-research.net/sigs/speech-sig/is15-compare`
Last retrieved 7/2/2015.

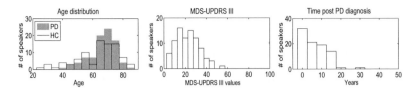

Figure 3.2: German – Distribution of age, UPDRS III values, and time post PD diagnosis.

3.2.1. Speech tasks

The recording protocol followed to built the German database includes also speech tasks to assess phonation, articulation, prosody, and intelligibility in speech of PD patients. Only the speech tasks that were used for this thesis are described below.

Sustained phonations

1. The sustained phonation of vowel /a/.

Diadochokinetic evaluation and isolated words

1. Rapid repetition of /pa-ta-ka/ (diadochokinetic evaluation).

2. Repetition of a set with six different isolated words: Bahnhofsvorsteher, Perlen-kettenschachtel, Bedienungsanleitung, Rettungsschwimmer, Toilettenpapier, and Bundes-gerichtshof.

Isolated sentences, read text, and spontaneous speech

1. Repetition of a set with 5 isolated sentences:

   a) Peter und Paul essen gerne Pudding.

   b) Das Fest war sehr gut vorbereitet.

   c) Seit seiner Hochzeit hat er sich sehr verändert.

   d) Im Inhaltsverzeichnis stand nichts über Lindenblütentee.

   e) Der Kerzenständer fiel gemeinsam mit der Blumenvase auf den Plattenspieler.

2. Reading of a text with 81 words:

   "Schildkröteninvasion: Von einer gewaltigen, von den Behörden geschütz-ten Invasion wird zur Zeit die Golf- und Pazifikküste Mexikos heimge-sucht: Wie alljährlich im Juni kommen Hunderttausende von Schildkröten aus dem Meer, um an Land ihre Eier abzulegen. Allein in der Nähe von Tampico wurden etwa 5000 Schildkröten beobachtet. Insgesamt wird in den kommenden Wochen mit einer Invasion von mehr als einer hal-ben Million Schildkröten gerechnet. Die mexikanischen Behörden lassen die Legeplätze sorgfältig bewachen, um den Diebstahl von Eiern zu ver-hindern und ausreichend Schildkrötennachwuchs sicherzustellen."

3. Spontaneous speech consisted in asking the speakers to talk about what they do during a normal day e.g., at what time do they used to wake up, which activities do they to during the day, at what time do they go to sleep. The average duration of monologues is 33 ± 8 seconds and 28 ± 6 seconds for PD and HC groups, respectively.

3.3. Czech

A total of 36 native Czech speakers were recorded (all were male), 20 of them were diagnosed with idiopathic PD and their age ranges from 41 to 60 (mean 61 ± 12). The age of the HC speakers range from 36 to 80 (mean 61.8 ± 13.3). The patients were evaluated by neurologist experts according to the UPDRS-III and Hoehn & Yahr scales and the average values are 17.9 ± 7.3 and 2.2 ± 0.5, respectively. All of the patients included in this database were newly diagnosed with PD, and none of them had been medicated before or during the recording session. The voice signals were sampled at 48 kHz with 16-bit resolution. The average duration of the disease prior to recording is 2.4 ± 1.7 years. Since the Czech participants were diagnosed with PD in the same moment of the recording session, this disease duration was obtained as a self report of patients according to the occurrence of the first motor impairment symptoms.

The distributions of the age, UPDRS-III, and the time post the diagnosis of the disease are illustrated in Figure 3.3.

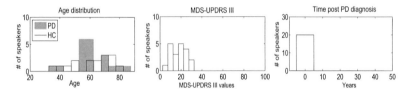

Figure 3.3: German – Distribution of age, UPDRS III values, and time post PD diagnosis.

3.3.1. Speech tasks

As in the case of German data, the Czech database includes speech tasks to assess phonation, articulation, and prosody in speech of PD patients. Only the speech tasks that were used for this thesis are described.

Sustained phonations

1. The sustained phonation of vowel /i/.

Diadochokinetic evaluation and isolated words

1. Rapid repetition of /pa-ta-ka/ (diadochokinetic evaluation).

2. Repetition of a set with twelve different isolated words: pepa, fouká, sada, tiká, kuká, chata, tři, vzhůru, sdružit, funkční, cukrářství, vstříc.

Isolated sentences, read text, and spontaneous speech

1. Repetition of a set with 3 isolated sentences:

   a) Kolik máte teď u sebe asi peněz?

   b) Kolikpak máte teďka u sebe asi peněz?

   c) Kolikpak máte teďka u sebe asi tak peněz?

2. Reading of a text with 80 words:

   "Když člověk po prvé vsadí do země sazeničku, chodí se na ni dívat třikrát denně: takco, povyrostla už nebo ne? I tají dech, naklání se nad ní, přitlačí trochu půdu u jejích kořínků, načechrává jí lístky a vůbec ji obtěžuje různým konáním, které považuje za užitecčnou péči. A když se sazenička přesto ujme a roste jako z vody, tu člověk žasne nad tímto divem přírody, má pocit čehosi jako zázraku a považuje to za jeden ze svých největších úspěchů."

3. Spontaneous speech: As in the German data, the speakers were asked to talk about what do they do during a normal day. The average duration of the monologues is 115 ± 56 seconds and 130 ± 51 seconds for PD and HC groups, respectively.

Chapter 4

Analysis of speech of patients with Parkinson's disease

The negative effects in speech of PD patients were described in Chapter 1. These symptoms are reflected in several impairments evidenced in different dimensions of speech. In this thesis three dimensions are studied: phonation, articulation, and prosody. For each dimension there are different methods to model the signal. The study of Parkinson's speech considering these three dimensions allows addressing several phenomena, for instance phonation analysis can give cues regarding the capability to control respiration and expel air from the lungs in order to make the vocal folds vibrate and produce vocal sounds. Articulation analysis can give information about the capability of patients to control the movement of several articulators to produce speech e.g., tongue, lips, jaw, and velum. Prosody analysis provides information about the intonation and timing in continuous speech; the lack of variability in vocal tone of PD patients is also modeled with this analysis. This chapter provides the description of several measurements calculated to model each of these three dimensions of speech. Additionally, as it was pointed out in chapter 1, one of the aims of the pathological speech analysis is to provide accurate methods to support the medical decisions of clinicians and therapists. In this thesis such decisions comprise two different tasks. The first one consists in discriminating between speech recordings of PD patients and healthy speakers, and the second one consists on predicting the neurological state of the patients according to the MDS-UPDRS-III scale. The binary decision i.e., Parkinson's patient vs. healthy speaker, is modeled here using a support vector machine with soft margin (SM-SVM), and the model for the estimation of the neurological state is built considering an ε-support vector regression (ε-SVR). Note that the main assumption for this modeling is that there is a strong correlation between the MDS-UPDRS-III label and the speech impairments suffered by the PD patients. The MDS-UPDRS-III scale is taken as the ground-truth reference because it is the global standard to assess PD patients; however, as it was pointed out in Chapter 2, this scale only considers the specific evaluation of speech in one of its 33 items.

The Chapter is distributed as follows. Section 4.1 describes the features that model the phonation process in speech; Section 4.2 includes the set of measurements to model articulation in speech signals; Section 4.3 describes the process for modeling the prosodic characteristics in speech; and finally Section 4.4 includes the description of the processes followed to take the decision whether a speech signal is from a PD patient and to estimate the neurological state of the patient according to the MDS-UPDRS-III scale.

4.1. Phonation analysis

Several phenomena can be studied to model the process of phonation during the production of voice signals. In this thesis three of them are considered including periodicity, noise content, and nonlinear behavior.

4.1.1. Periodicity

Periodicity in speech involves the ability to generate constant airflow during the production of sustained vowels [Alon 05]. The stability of such airflow coming out through the vocal folds can be modeled considering amplitude and/or frequency variations.

Fundamental frequency of voice – F_0: It is associated to the vibration period of the vocal folds and its perceptual impression is called pitch[1] [Resc 07]. There are several methods to compute F_0, one of the most common is calculating the autocorrelation function of the voice signal, eliminating its negative part i.e., clipping, and taking the distance between the first two peaks of the autocorrelation function [Boer 93].

Short-term amplitude and temporal variation of F_0: These two variations are classically used to analyze stability of the fundamental frequency. The voice signal $x(n)$ is divided into voice frames x_i with maximum amplitude $A[x_i]$, the variation of those amplitude values is called shimmer and it is defined as

$$\text{Shimmer}[x_i](\%) = 100 \times \frac{|A[x_i] - A[x_{i-1}]|}{\overline{A}}, \tag{4.1}$$

where $\overline{A}$ is the average value of the maximum amplitude measured in the previous three voice frames i.e., $A[x_{i-1}]$, $A[x_{i-2}]$, and $A[x_{i-3}]$. The temporal variation of the fundamental frequency is called jitter. For a voice frame x_i with fundamental frequency $F_0[x_i]$, it is defined as

$$\text{Jitter}[x_i](\%) = 100 \times \frac{|F_0[x_i] - F_0[x_{i-1}]|}{\overline{F_0}}, \tag{4.2}$$

were $\overline{F_0}$ is the average value of the fundamental frequency measured in the previous three voice frames.

Long-term stability of voice frames: The stability of sustained phonations in long-term voice frames can be analyzed with different measurements. This thesis includes the pitch perturbation quotient (PPQ), which is used to measure the variability of the pitch period evaluated in five consecutive voice cycles. The long-term stability of the amplitude is considered with the amplitude perturbation quotient (APQ), which is the average difference between the amplitude value of five preceding pitch periods and their respective five successive values. The perturbation of the pitch period is also quantified using the relative average perturbation (RAP), which measures the difference between period-to-period in a phonation and evaluates whether the period duration is smoothed over three adjacent voice cycles [Boya 97].

---

[1]F_0 and pitch are often used as synonyms in the literature.

Figure 4.1 shows the pitch contour estimated from a sustained phonation produced by two female speakers with similar ages. PD patient (left side) shows instabilities in the contour, exhibiting clear signs of hypokinetic dysarthria, while the healthy speaker does not show signs of uncontrolled changes in the contour.

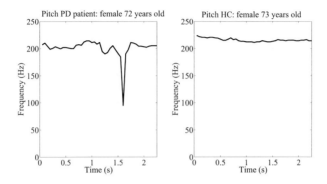

Figure 4.1: Pitch contour estimated from sustained phonations.

4.1.2. Noise content

Noise in speech appears mainly due to incomplete closure of the vocal folds [Kasu 86]. As people with PD develop uncontrolled movement of vocal folds, a detailed modeling of this phenomenon may help to understand the impact of the disease in speech. A set with six noise measures is considered in this work.

Harmonics to Noise Ratio (HNR): This measure is based on the assumption that the acoustic wave of a sustained vowel has two components, a periodic component which is similar from cycle to cycle and an additive noise component that should has a zero-mean amplitude distribution. The concatenation of the periodic components produces a new signal which energy is estimated. The energy of the noise is estimated as the subtraction of the energy of the concatenated signal from the original one. HNR is defined as the ratio between the energy of the Harmonic structure of the signal and the additive noise that appears due to voice impairments [Yumo 82].

Cepstral version of HNR (CHNR): The measurement of HNR in the cepstral domain considers all the spectral components of speech, improving the precision of the noise levels estimation. The voice signal $x(n)$ is divided into several voice frames x_i whose duration is a pitch period. Such intervals are windowed and then the cepstrum C_{x_i} is calculated. In the cepstral domain the harmonics are filtered (this process is called "liftering" when it is applied upon the cepstral domain). The Fourier transform of the signal after the liftering process is calculated to find the noise spectrum N_i. The harmonic spectrum is calculated as the subtraction of $\log N_i$ from the logarithm of the spectrum of the voice frame x_i. In order to make a more accurate estimation of the noise level, the minimum values between successive harmonics and the harmonic spectrum are found and grouped into the vector

mH_i. The noise spectrum N_i is subtracted from mH_i, to estimate the noise level in the signal. Finally, CHNR is the ratio between the absolute value of the spectrum of the voice frame x_i and the corrected noise level [Murp 05].

Voice Turbulence Index (VTI): This measure is an average ratio of the energy in the non-harmonic part of the voice spectrum between 2800 Hz and 5800 Hz and the harmonic energy between 70 Hz to 4500 Hz. According to previous observations, VTI measures correlate with turbulences caused by incomplete or loose adduction of the vocal folds [Di N 06].

Soft Phonation Index (SPI): This measure quantifies the harmonic structure of the spectrum. It is an average ratio of the harmonic energy in the frequency interval between 70 Hz and 1600 Hz to the harmonic energy between 1600 Hz and 4500 Hz. This measure gives also cues regarding the adduction process of vocal folds [Di N 06]. SPI is very sensitive to the vowel formant structure, thus it can also be considered an articulation measure. In this thesis it is included in the set of phonation measures.

Normalized Noise Energy (NNE): To compute this feature it is assumed that a voice frame x_i whose duration is equivalent to a pitch period, can be represented by the sum of a periodic component s_i and additive noise w_i i.e., $x_i(n) = s_i(n) + w_i(n)$. NNE is defined as the ratio between the energy of the noise w_i and the energy of the signal x_i. The energy of the noise is estimated as the sum of contributions of non-harmonic portions of the voice spectrum i.e., deep regions in the spectrum [Kasu 86].

Glottal to Noise Excitation (GNE): It quantifies the amount of excitation in voice during the vibration of the vocal folds relative to the excitation noise due to turbulences in the vocal tract [Mich 97]. In this case the voice signal is re-sampled at 10 kHz and the glottal pulses are found by a linear predictive inverse filtering. The signal with the glottal pulses is filtered by a set of band-pass filters with bandwidths increasing in steps of 300 Hz. The Hilbert envelope is calculated through all of the band-passed intervals. The cross-correlation among all of the intervals is estimated and its maximum value is defined as the GNE [Mich 97].

4.1.3. Nonlinear behavior

Previous observations confirm different nonlinear phenomena in voice signals including nonlinear pressure-flow in the glottis, nonlinear stress-strain curves of vocal folds tissues, and nonlinear vocal fold collision [Herz 94]. Additionally, there is a nonlinear behavior in speech when the speaker makes compensatory movements in different muscles and limbs of the vocal tract. Such movements appear when the speaker realizes that he/she is speaking inappropriately and tries to correct the "errors" while talking [Gold 01]. To model those nonlinear phenomena the voice signal is represented in the state space according to the embedding procedure. Once the signal is embedded, several nonlinear dynamic features can be estimated from such representation.

Embedding procedure: As the voice production system is nonlinear, it can be described using a set of nonlinear differential equations $\dot{X}(t) = f\{X(t)\}$ such that the relationship f among the variables of the system is represented by nonlinear vector functions. The set $X(t) = [\chi_1(t), \chi_2(t)..., \chi_\varsigma(t)]$ is the state vector composed by ς state variables, where ς corresponds to the number of first order differential equations required to describe the dynamics of the system. The solutions of the differential equations describing a system generate a set of trajectories in the state space which are called *attractor* [Kant 06]. When the f function that describes the system is unknown, the state space can be reconstructed from the output of the system which in our case is the voice signal $x(n)$. The state space is reconstructed applying the embedding theorem originally proposed in [Take 81]. It allows the reconstruction of diffeomorphic attractors, i.e., those that hold the topological properties (qualitative) of the system. According to the theorem, an embedded discrete signal is represented as

$$\mathbf{x}(k) = \{x(k), x(k + \tau), x(k + 2\tau), ..., x(k + (\vartheta - 1)\tau)\}, \quad (4.3)$$

where $\mathbf{x} = \{\mathbf{x}(k)\}$ is the set of points in the attractor, $k = 1, 2, ..., l$ and $l = N - (\vartheta - 1)\tau$; N is the number of points in the time series e.g., the length of a voice frame $x_i(n)$, ϑ and τ are two parameters required for the embedding process. ϑ corresponds to the dimension of the embedding space and τ is the time delay estimated to assure minimum correlation among the state variables.

The embedding dimension ϑ is estimated according to the *false neighbors method* [Kenn 92], which is based on the assumption of a minimum embedding dimension ϑ_0 to reconstruct the topological properties of the attractor of the time series $x_i(n)$. Surrounding each embedded point, there will be a set of neighbors whose number will depend on the neighborhood size. If we suppose that the series $x_i(n)$ is embedded in a space R^ϑ such that $\vartheta < \vartheta_0$, the topological features of the attractor are destroyed because the new space is a projection of the previous one R^{ϑ_0}, thus there will be points projected into wrong neighborhoods which originally belonged to other spaces with higher dimensionality. Such points are called *false neighbors*.

For the estimation of the time delay τ, a method based on the mutual information is applied [Fras 86]. This estimation consists on finding the first minimum of the auto-mutual information of the signal $x_i(n)$, and it is defined as

$$I(T) = \sum\nolimits_{n=1}^{N} P(x(n), x(n + T)) \log_2 \frac{P(x(n), x(n + T))}{P(x(n))P(x(n + T))}, \quad (4.4)$$

where $P(x(n), x(n+T))$ is the probability to observe $x(n)$ and $x(n+T)$ on the same time, and $P(x(n))$ is the probability to observe $x(n)$. $I(T)$ is an information measure of $x(n)$ when $x(n + T)$ is observed and the value of the delay can be found when the value $T = \tau$ is the first local minimum of $I(T)$.

The nonlinear dynamics (NLD) features are developed to model irregularities in the reconstructed attractors. According to [Jian 06] the more pathological is the phonation, the more irregular are the trajectories of the reconstructed attractor. Figure 4.2 shows the attractors reconstructed from sustained phonations performed by two speakers, one PD patient (left) and one healthy control (right). Note that the trajectories of the HC attractor seem to be more regular and to follow some pattern, while the trajectories of the PD attractor are more irregular.

Once the voice signal is embedded in the state space, several NLD features can be estimated from the reconstructed attractor.

Correlation dimension (D_2): It is a measure of the space dimensionality occupied by the points of the reconstructed attractor. D_2 is calculated according to the Takens estimator

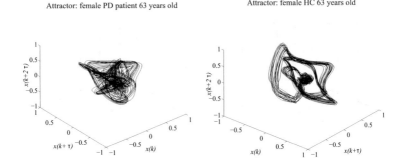

Figure 4.2: Reconstructed attractor from sustained phonations of the Spanish vowel /a/.

method [Kant 06]. Such estimation requires the correlation sum $C(r)$, which is defined as $C(r) = \sum_{i=1}^{N_\vartheta} C_i^\vartheta(r)$ and

$$C_i^\vartheta(r) = \frac{2}{N_\vartheta(N_\vartheta - 1)} \sum_{j=i+1}^{N_\vartheta} \Theta(r - ||\mathbf{x}_i - \mathbf{x}_j||), \tag{4.5}$$

where Θ is the Heaviside function, $\mathbf{x}_i$ and $\mathbf{x}_j$ are points from the trajectories in the reconstructed attractor ($i \neq j \in \{1, 2, ..., N_\vartheta\}$), r is the defined radius of a hypersphere around which the points are counted by Θ, N_ϑ is the number of points in the state space, and $||\cdot||$ is a norm defined in any consistent metric space. D_2 is theoretically defined for an infinity amount of data ($N_\vartheta \to \infty$) and for a small r, thus its general expression is written as

$$D_2 = \lim_{r \to 0} \lim_{N_\vartheta \to \infty} \frac{\partial \ln C(r, N_\vartheta)}{\partial \ln (r)}. \tag{4.6}$$

The r value could be fixed at $r = r_c \times \text{std}(x_i(n))$, where $r_c = 0.35$ and $\text{std}(x_i(n))$ is the standard deviation of the voice frame $x_i(n)$. The value $r_c = 0.35$ was optimized for voice signals in [Aria 11].

Largest Lyapunov exponent (LLE): this feature represents the average divergence rate of neighbor trajectories in the state space, thus it is closely related with the predictability of a dynamical system, then abnormal behavior in its dynamics can be modeled using this measurement. It is estimated according to the Ronsenstein's method [Kant 06]. The nearest neighbors to every point in the trajectories need to be estimated. Only neighbors with a temporal separation greater than the "period" of the time series are considered. According to the Oseledec's theorem [Osel 68] it is possible to state that the separation of points in a trajectory is according to the expression $d(t) = \gamma e^{\lambda_1 t}$, where λ_1 is the maximum Lyapunov exponent, $d(t)$ is the average divergence taken at the time t, and γ is a normalization constant. If the $\kappa - th$ pair of nearest neighbors approximately diverge at a rate of λ_1, then $\ln [d_\kappa(i)] = \ln (\gamma_\kappa) + \lambda_1(i \Delta t)$, where λ_1 is the slope of the average line that appears when such expression is drawn on a logarithmic plane [Kant 06].

Lempel-Ziv complexity (LZC): It is classically used to estimate the complexity of computer algorithms, and it can also be used for estimating complexity in discrete time series [Kasp 87]. The algorithm consists on finding the number of different "patterns" in a given binary sequence. For the practical case, a 0 is assigned when the difference between two successive samples is negative and a 1 is assigned when the difference is positive or null. The estimation of LZC is based on the reconstruction of a sequence $\mathbf{B}_x$ by means of the copying and insertion of symbols in a new sequence. Given the binary sequence $\mathbf{B} = B_1, B_2, \ldots, B_n$, it is analyzed from left to right, the first bit is taken by default as the initial point. A variable S is defined to store the bits that have been inserted i.e., at the beginning S only has B_1. The variable Q is defined for the accumulation of bits that have been analyzed from left to right in the bit stream. On each iteration, the union of S and Q, denoted by SQ is generated. When the sequence Q does not belong to the string $SQ\pi$, which is the result of eliminating the last bit of the stream SQ, the insertion of bits in the subset of symbols finishes. The value of LZC is the number of subsets used for the representation of the original signal [Lemp 76].

Hurst exponent (H): The possible long term dependencies in a time series can be estimated through H. It is calculated following the rank scaling method [Kant 06], where the relation between the variation rank (R) of the signal, evaluated in a segment, and its standard deviation υ is given by $\frac{R}{\upsilon} = cN^H$, where c is a scaling constant, N is the duration of the segment and H is the Hurst exponent.

Entropy-based measurements: Entropy is a measure of uncertainty of a random variable. When there is a stochastic process with a set of independent but not identically distributed variables X_i, the rate at which the joint entropy grows with the number of variables ζ is given by $H(X) = -\lim\limits_{\zeta \to \infty} \frac{1}{\zeta} \sum\limits_{i=1}^{\zeta} H(X_i)$.

For the case of a state space, it can be partitioned into hypercubes of content ε^ϑ and observed at time intervals δ, defining the Kolmogorov-Sinai entropy as

$$H_{KS} = -\lim_{\substack{\delta \to \infty \\ \varepsilon \to 0 \\ \zeta \to \infty}} \frac{1}{\zeta \delta} \sum_{k_1, \ldots, k_\zeta} p(k_1, \ldots, k_\zeta) \log p(k_1, \ldots, k_\zeta), \qquad (4.7)$$

where $p(k_1, \ldots, k_\zeta)$ is the joint probability that the state of the system is in the hypercube k_1 at the time $t = \delta$, k_2 at $t = 2\delta$, etc. For stationary processes, it can be shown that $H_{KS} = \lim\limits_{\delta \to 0} \lim\limits_{\varepsilon \to 0} \lim\limits_{\zeta \to \infty} (H_{\zeta+1} - H_\zeta)$.

In practical terms it is not possible to compute the equation 4.7 for $\zeta \to \infty$, thus different estimation methods have been proposed in the literature. One of them is the *Approximate entropy* (A_E), which is designed for measuring the average conditional information generated by diverging points on a trajectory in the state space [Cost 05]. For fixed values of ϑ and r, A_E is estimated as

$$A_E(\vartheta, r) = \lim_{N_\vartheta \to \infty} \left[\Upsilon^{\vartheta+1}(r) - \Upsilon^\vartheta(r) \right], \qquad (4.8)$$

where $\Upsilon^\vartheta(r) = \frac{1}{N_\vartheta - \vartheta + 1} \sum\limits_{i=1}^{N_\vartheta - \vartheta + 1} \ln C_i^\vartheta(r)$, and $C_i^\vartheta(r)$ was defined in equation 4.5.

The main drawback of A_E is its dependence to the signal length due to the self comparison of points in the attractor. In order to overcome this problem, the *sample entropy* (S_E) is proposed in [Rich 00] as

$$S_E\left(\vartheta, r\right) = \lim_{N_\vartheta \to \infty} \left(-\ln \frac{\Gamma^{\vartheta+1}(r)}{\Gamma^\vartheta(r)}\right).\tag{4.9}$$

The only difference between Γ in the equation 4.9 and Υ in the equation 4.8 is that the first one does not compare embedding vectors with themselves.

A_E is also modified into the *approximate entropy with Gaussian kernel* A_EGK. With a Gaussian kernel function greater weights are assigned to nearby points by replacing the Heaviside function by $d_G(\mathbf{x}_i, \mathbf{x}_j)$ [Xu 05].

$$d_G\left(\mathbf{x}_i, \mathbf{x}_j\right) = \exp\left(-\frac{(||\mathbf{x}_i - \mathbf{x}_j||_1)}{10r^2}\right)\tag{4.10}$$

Where $||\cdot||_1$ represents the L_1-norm. The same procedure of changing the distance measure can be applied to define the *sample entropy with Gaussian kernel* S_EGK.

Measures based on the recurrence and fractal-scaling analysis in embedded attractors: As it was already mentioned in Chapter 1, further to the aforementioned measurements, in 2009 Little et al. introduced a couple of novel nonlinear parameters which are also measured from the reconstructed attractor of the voice signal i.e., RPDE and the scaling exponent of the DFA [Litt 07]. Such measures have been used in several studies with sustained phonations of PD speakers and they have been also tested in this thesis. The main assumption for their application is that the voice signal has two components, deterministic and stochastic. The deterministic component is analyzed by the RPDE considering a hypersphere of radius $r > 0$, containing an embedded data point $\mathbf{x}(k_j)$. The time $k_r = k_j - k_i$ is the recurrence time, where k_j is the instant at which the trajectory first returned to the same hypersphere. If $R(t)$ is the normalized histogram of the recurrence times estimated for all embedded points into a reconstructed attractor, the RPDE can be defined as

$$\text{RPDE} = \frac{-\sum_{i=1}^{t_{max}} R(i) \ln R(i)}{\ln t_{max}},\tag{4.11}$$

where t_{max} is the maximum recurrence time in the attractor.

The stochastic component of the voice signal is modeled by the scaling exponent β of the DFA, which is calculated integrating the voice frame as $y(n) = \sum_{i=1}^n x_i$, where $n = 1, 2, \ldots, N$. $y(n)$ is divided into frames with L samples. The root-mean-squared error, defined as

$$F(L) = \left[\frac{1}{L}\sum_{n=1}^{L}(y(n) - a_n - b)^2\right]^{\frac{1}{2}},\tag{4.12}$$

is computed between each integrated frame $y(n)$ and the least-square straight-line that is optimized on each frame considering the parameters a_n and b. The process is repeated for all of the frames with L samples length. The $\log L$ vs. $\log F(L)$ plane is built and the line on the plane, which indicates self-similarity, can be expressed as the proportionality $F(L)\alpha L^\beta$. The DFA corresponds to a sigmoid normalization of the scaling exponent β.

Teager Energy Operator – TEO: This is a nonlinear operator that is useful to model multi-component signals i.e., signals that result as the combination of several components. For a discrete signal $x(n)$ TEO is defined as [Cair 96]

$$\Psi[x(n)] = x(n)^2 - x(n+1)x(n-1), \tag{4.13}$$

where n can be any discrete independent variable. Note that the TEO does not obey the superposition principle, which means that if a signal $x(n)$ is expressed by the sum of two independent and uncorrelated components such that $x(n) = s(n)+g(n)$, the resulting TEO is given by

$$\Psi[x(n)] = \Psi[s(n)] + \Psi[g(n)] + \Psi_{cross}[s(n), g(n)]\Psi_{cross}[g(n), s(n)] \tag{4.14}$$

where $\Psi_{cross}[s(n), g(n)] = g(n)s(n) - g(n+1)s(n-1)$ appears due to the existence of multiple components in $x(n)$.

The spectrum of a hypernasal speech signal is characterized to be a multi-component signal, since it comprises vocal resonances of the normal speech, and also additional nasal resonances that appear due to the pathology [Cair 96]. The articulatory problems observed in the speech of PD patients include the uncontrolled movement of the velum. Such impairment leads some of the patients to increase the nasal airflow emission while speaking i.e., hypernasal speech.

The sensitivity of the TEO to multiple-component signals can be exploited to model hypernasal speech. The main assumption is that if the first formant of a voice signal is filtered with a band-pass filter, the resulting spectrum will be a single-component signal even in the case of voice signals with excess of nasalization. Conversely, if a low-pass filter is applied, one would expect that the result of hypernasal signals will contain multiple components i.e., the first formant along with the nasal-formant and the anti-formant [Bela 13]. Considering such effect, different measurements that quantify the difference between the TEO of the filtered signals are used in this thesis to model the problems of PD patients to control the velum. Note that this operator could be part of the set of articulation measurements; however, in this thesis it is included in the set of nonlinear features due to its nonlinear nature.

4.2. Articulation analysis

Articulation is a dimension of speech that reflects the ability of a speaker to move and put the articulators in the correct position, on the correct time, and with the appropriate duration and energy while producing speech. This dimension is key to produce intelligible continuous speech and it is affected in patients with PD. The evaluation of articulation in PD patients is performed typically by means of the vocal space and the spectral and cepstral analyses. In this thesis these two aspects are considered and additionally, a new approach based on the automatic separation of voiced and unvoiced frames is proposed.

4.2.1. Vocal space

Vowels are produced mainly by movements of the tongue, lips, and jaw, creating several resonance cavities that have a certain frequency response at a certain frequency bands. The harmonics in such frequency response are called "formants". The first two formants, F_1 and F_2, are used for modeling vocal sounds e.g., vowels, and some times to infer the position of the articulators.

As the movement of the articulators is impaired in PD speakers, one can expect that the vowels they produce have altered amplitude and frequency values of F_1 and F_2. The alterations in frequency can be represented in the F_1 vs. F_2 plane i.e., vocal space. Typically the three vowels /a/, /i/, and /u/ are represented in the vocal space. The area of the triangle formed by these three vowel in the space is called triangular vowel space (tVSA). This measure provides information about the articulatory capability of a speaker, and it has been used to assess articulation in PD patients [Skod 11c].

Figure 4.3 shows the difference of the vocal triangle obtained from three different PD patients with respect to the average vocal triangle built with phonations of 50 age-matched healthy speakers.

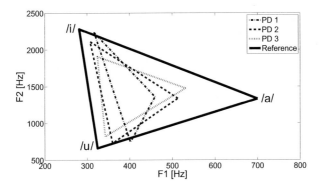

Figure 4.3: Triangular vowel space.

A similar analysis can be made considering the five Spanish vowels to build the "vocal pentagon" also in the F_1 vs. F_2 plane. Figure 4.4 illustrates the difference between the average pentagon obtained with recordings of the 50 healthy speakers of GITA-PC and the pentagon obtained for one PD patient. The vocal pentagon area (VPA) can be used also to model the articulatory capability of people when recordings of the five Spanish vowels are available.

Another feature that can be derived from the vocal space is the Formant Centralization Ratio (FCR), which has been successfully used for the modeling of dysarthric speech signals [Sapi 10]. This ratio is defined as

$$FCR = \frac{F_1/i/ + F_1/u/ + F_2/u/ + F_2/a/}{F_2/i/ + F_1/a/}, \tag{4.15}$$

where $F_1/a/$, $F_1/i/$, and $F_1/u/$ are the frequency of the first formant of the vowels /a/, /i/, and /u/. Similarly, $F_2/a/$, $F_2/i/$, and $F_2/u/$ are the frequency of the second formant of the vowels /a/, /i/, and /u/, respectively.

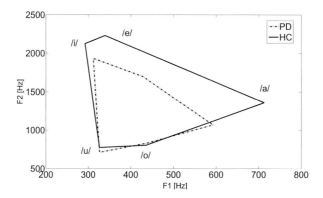

Figure 4.4: Vocal pentagon.

4.2.2. Spectral-Cepstral analysis

According to the reviewed literature in Chapter 1, the speech spectrum has been studied mainly using measures of the formant frequencies which provide explicit and well documented information about the position of the tongue, jaw, and lips [Sapi 10]. However, they are not robust against nasalization and noise in speech. Using spectral and/or cepstral coefficients to evaluate vowels it is also possible to obtain information about articulators; although such information is not as explicit as when formants are calculated, those coefficients allow modeling the vocal tract robustly. Additionally, using spectral or cepstral coefficients it is possible to obtain more detailed information of the speech spectrum and they can be used not only to study vocal sounds but also consonants and stops [Hall 57]. Different techniques and procedures have been applied in this thesis in order to model the speech spectrum. Several details about the methods are presented below.

Linear Prediction Coefficients – LPC: This technique comprises an all-pole representation of speech signals. It is assumed that a signal $x(n)$ is produced by a linear system i.e., the vocal tract, with transfer function given by

$$H(z) = \frac{G}{1 + \sum_{k=1}^{p} a_k z^{-k}}, \tag{4.16}$$

where G is the gain of the system, a_k are the linear prediction coefficients (LPCs), and p is the number of coefficients.

LPCs have been used in several applications including formant extraction, speech coding, and speech recognition, among others. The technique has proven to be useful for articulation analysis in speech of people with PD because these patients are unable to have a total motor control of their vocal tract, altering the frequency response of the filter used to model it [Rusz 11]. Additionally, most of the people with PD develop problems to control the velum and LPC coefficients have demonstrated to be sensitive to the presence of nasalization in speech, thus LPC modeling may be used to evaluate excess of nasalization due to inappropriate velopharyngeal function of people with PD [Kent 99].

Linear Prediction Cepstral Coefficients – LPCC: Given the set of LPC coefficients $\{a_k\}$, the Cepstrum of such set that represents the vocal tract filter comprises the LPCCs which can be calculated as

$$\text{LPCC}_i = a_i + \sum_{k=1}^{i-1} \left(\frac{k-i}{i}\right) \text{LPCC}_{i-k} a_k. \tag{4.17}$$

LPCCs have demonstrated to be more robust than LPCs in several speech recognition tasks [Kim 00].

Mel-frequency Cepstral Coefficients – MFCC: These are the standard measures for speech recognition and have been tested in several speaker recognition tasks and in modeling different kind of pathologies such as dysphonia [Godi 06, Aria 10], hypernasality [Maie 09, Muri 11], and dysarthria [Bock 13, Rusz 11], among others. The estimation of the MFCCs consists on taking the Discrete Cosine Transform (DCT) of the log-energy which frequencies are equally spaced along the mel-scale. This procedure is summarized in the following equation [Davi 80]:

$$\text{MFCC}_i = \sum_{k=1}^{N} X_k cos \left[i\left(k-\frac{1}{2}\right)\frac{\pi}{N}\right] \quad i = 1, 2, ..., M. \tag{4.18}$$

Where M is the number of cepstrum coefficients, X_k, $k = 1, 2, ..., N$ is the log-energy output of the k-th triangular band-pass filter, and N is the number of filters. The distribution of the frequencies of the triangular filters is according to the mel-scale which is given by

$$\text{Mel}_f = 2595 \ln\left(1 + \frac{f}{700}\right), \tag{4.19}$$

where f is the frequency in Hertz and M_f is the Mel-frequency in [Mels].

MFCCs comprise a compact representation of the short term spectrum. Such compression is adapted to the human hearing achieving a perceptual modeling of the speech spectrum. Previous studies have shown that MFCCs can model irregular movements in vocal tract [Godi 06] which supports their suitability to analyze PD speech.

Perceptual Linear Prediction Coefficients – PLP: These coefficients are a version of LPCCs which includes perceptually adequate compression. They are nearly equivalent to MFCCs but include an additional smoothing step [Honi 05]. These coefficients have been designed to model the vocal tract in different frequency bands i.e., critical bands, which are scaled according to a model of the human auditory system [Herm 90]. The LPC analysis assumes the same number of resonances on every frequency bands; however, there is evidence demonstrating that beyond about 800 Hz, the spectral resolution of hearing decreases with frequency [Herm 90]. As this approach suggests a more accurate modeling of the speech spectrum, one can expect more robust results with PLPs than with other techniques like LPC or LPCC. However, in [Oroz 15a] it is demonstrated that LPCC are more suitable for Parkinson's disease detection than others perceptual coefficients like PLP.

Relative Spectra Coefficients – RASTA: Assuming that human perception is less sensitive to slowly varying stimuli, which makes the speech analysis less sensitive to slowly changing factors, Hynek Hermansky proposed these coefficients [Herm 94]. The model replaces the critical-band filter of the PLP modeling by a filter-bank with a sharp spectral zero at the border frequency. RASTA modeling includes a filtering in the time domain that removes low and high frequencies corresponding to static channel properties and noise, respectively [Herm 94]. RASTA coefficients can be represented in spectral or in cepstral domain, each approach is called RASTA-SPEC and RASTA-CEPS, respectively. The difference between both approaches is the linear transformation that is performed in RASTA-CEPS.

Group Delay Functions – GDF: They are applied to improve the resolution of the low frequency zone in the speech spectrum and are defined as $\tau(f) = -\frac{\partial \theta(f)}{\partial f}$. For discrete-time signals the expression becomes into [Murt 91]

$$\tau(\omega) = \frac{X(\omega)_R Y(\omega)_R + X(\omega)_I Y(\omega)_I}{|X(\omega)|^2}, \qquad (4.20)$$

where ω is the discrete frequency and $X(\omega)$ and $Y(\omega)$ are the N-point Discrete Fourier Transform (DFT) of the sequences $x(n)$ and $nx(n)$, respectively. The subscripts R and I denote the real and imaginary parts of the DFT, respectively.

To reduce the spiky nature of the GDF, which is due to the pitch peaks, noise, and windowing effects, the original function is modified to define the Modified Group Delay Function (MGDF) as [Vija 07]

$$\text{MGDF}(\omega) = \text{sign} \left| \frac{X(\omega)_R Y(\omega)_R + X(\omega)_I Y(\omega)_I}{S(\omega)^{2\sigma}} \right|^\alpha, \qquad (4.21)$$

where $0 < \{\alpha, \sigma\} < 1$, $S(\omega)^2$ is a cepstrally smoothed version of $|X(\omega)|^2$, and sign is the sign obtained from the equation 4.20.

To improve the resolution of the spectrum, the voice signal is low-pass filtered and the MGDF is calculated from the spectrum to estimate the first two formants. The amplitude of the first formant will be lower in speech signals with excess of nasalization than in healthy ones, thus it is possible to define an index of nasalization called Group Delay function-based Acoustic Measure (GDAM) as [Vija 07]

$$\text{GDAM} = \frac{|\text{MGDF}(F_1)|}{|\text{MGDF}(F_2)|}. \qquad (4.22)$$

4.2.3. Voiced-Unvoiced modeling

As it was already described in Chapter 1, the speech of PD patients is characterized for its imprecise production of stop consonants such as /p/, /t/, /k/, /b/, and /g/ [Loge 81]. Inappropriate tongue elevation, abnormal oropharyngeal movements, and reduced energy when producing consonant sounds have been observed as well [Robb 86, Gobe 08]. Additionally, in [Mera 05] the authors state that PD patients, as other people suffering from movement disorders affecting the larynx, can develop abductor spasms typically occurring during the production of unvoiced sounds.

The clinical evidence suggests that the modeling of consonant sounds is suitable to assess PD speech; however, the research community has mainly used the unvoiced sounds to detect the onset and offset of syllables and words [Chen 11, Noth 11]. In this thesis the energy content of the unvoiced frames is measured with several techniques in order to model the impaired production of consonant sounds. The main hypothesis that motivates the modeling of unvoiced frames in PD speech is:

PD patients produce abnormal unvoiced sounds and have difficulty to begin and/or to stop the vocal fold vibration. It can be observed on speech signals by modeling the frequency content of the unvoiced frames and the transitions between voiced and unvoiced sounds.

The process to validate this hypothesis consists on the automatic segmentation of voiced and unvoiced frames. In this thesis, voiced frames are defined as the portion of a speech recording where there is detected a pitch value and unvoiced frames are those where there is no detected pitch. The minimum duration of the voiced frames to be processed is 40 ms and the maximum duration of the unvoiced frames is 270 ms (longer unvoiced frames are considered pauses). These lower and upper limits have been tuned manually by direct observation during several experiments. Two different approaches are designed. The first one consists on calculating the energy content of the voiced/unvoiced frames separately (Figure 4.5 part a) and the second one consists calculating the energy of the transitions between voiced/unvoiced and unvoiced/voiced (Figure 4.5 part b). Note that the second approach reflects the processes to stop and to start the vocal fold vibration which are two of the difficulties observed by clinicians in PD patients.

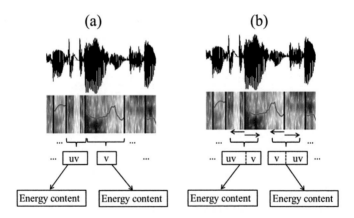

Figure 4.5: Modeling of the processes to start/stop the vocal fold vibration.

The energy content can be quantified by several methods. In this thesis the MFCCs have been calculated along with the energy distributed according to the Bark-band scale[2]. The MFCCs are calculated as it was described in Section 4.2.2. The energies in Bark-band scale are calculated according to the original procedure proposed by Zwicker et al. in [Zwic 57]. The Bark scale is motivated in the concept of *critical bands*, which refers to frequency regions that reflect the excitation of the basilar membrane when it is stimulated by specific frequencies. The boundaries of the critical bands depend upon specific stimuli and were established empirically through several experiments [Zwic 57]. According to [Zwic 80] for frequencies below 500 Hz the bandwidths of the critical bands are constant at 100 Hz

---

[2]The word Bark comes from the name of the inventor of the unit of loudness level, Prof. Heinrich Georg Barkhausen.

while for medium and high frequencies the increment is proportional to the logarithm of frequency. The Equation 4.23 reproduces the frequency distribution proposed by Zwicker et al. with an accuracy of ± 0.2 Bark.

$$\text{Bark}(f) = 13 \arctan\left(0.76\frac{f}{\text{kHz}}\right) + 3.5 \arctan\left(\frac{f}{7.5\,\text{kHz}}\right)^2, \qquad (4.23)$$

arctan is measured in [radians] and f is in [kHz].

4.3. Prosody analysis

The proper timing and intonation are necessary to produce intelligible and natural speech. The evaluation of prosodic features have captured special interest in the research community since several years ago due to their suitability to assess the production of natural speech [Noth 02, Zeis 06, Schu 11]. The prosody analysis allows modeling changes in the intonation, timing, and loudness in speech. These characteristics have been successfully used to detect/assess emotional speech [Stei 09, Schu 11, Schu 15]. As it was described in Section 2.2, people with Parkinson's disease are characterized for exhibiting a monotonic speech and for showing difficulty to change its loudness. Additionally, the non-motor symptoms of PD patients include depression, anxiety, and apathy mood, among others [Mart 11, Sotg 13]. The analysis of prosody in speech of people with PD could provide additional clues regarding the neurological state of the person. This approach has been successfully used for telemedical therapy of people with dysarthric speech [Noth 11] and has been highlighted by Neurologists as a promising bio-marker to assess Parkinson's disease [Skod 13].

The Chair of Pattern Recognition has wide experience in the analysis of prosody in speech e.g., published in [Hade 15, Stei 09, Batl 03, Hube 02, Gall 02, Noth 00]. Additionally, the Chair has developed the *Erlangen Prosody Module* during the VERMOBIL [Batl 00] and SMARTKOM [Wahl 06] projects.

Before introducing the prosodic features that had been calculated in this thesis, it is necessary to define the context of their computation i.e., the speech intervals over which the features are calculated. Prosodic features are able to characterize suprasegmental phenomena in speech frames larger than phonemes i.e., syllables, words, phrases, or turns which are defined as speech frames between pauses of at least one second long [Noth 99, Stei 09]. Most of the methods applied and proposed in this thesis were chosen with the aim of performing a language-independent processing of the Parkinsonian speech signals, thus the speech units defined for the prosodic analysis here are based on the voiced/unvoiced segmentation, instead of words or syllables, which have been the typical speech units defined to extract prosodic features. The context used in this thesis for the computation of the local prosodic features comprises two different options, (1) the current unit is a voiced frame and it is considered from its beginning until its end i.e., (0,0), and (2) is the speech chunk that results of joining the current and the next speech unit until its final point i.e., (0,1). Figure 4.6 illustrates these two speech units defined for one part of the sentence *"Omar, que vive cerca, trajo miel"*. Note that there are another studies where longer contexts are taken e.g.,(-1,1) or (1,2), which means to consider analysis frames from the beginning of the previous speech unit until the end of the next one, or from the beginning of the next one until the end of the second one, respectively [Hade 07, Stei 09].

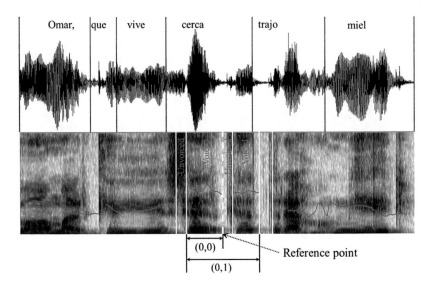

Figure 4.6: Context and speech units processed with the Prosody Module.

The features of the Erlangen Prosody Module can be grouped into three subsets, one to model the contour of the fundamental frequency (F_0), another one to model the short-term energy, and the third one to model temporal aspects of the analyzed speech frames. The next sections describe each group of features and the contexts where they are calculated.

4.3.1.   Features based on the fundamental frequency

The F_0-based features allow modeling the contour of the fundamental frequency. The set of measures extracted from the F_0 contour (in logarithmic scale) includes local features i.e., calculated in the defined contexts (0,0) or (0,1), and global features, which are computed for intervals of up to 15 consecutive speech units as in [Hade 15]. The local features include the regression coefficient and the mean square error (MSE) of the F_0 curve calculated with respect to the regression curve; the values and position of the minimum and the maximum of F_0; the value and position of F_0 in the onset and offset, and the values and variance of jitter and shimmer. The set with the global features comprises the average value and the standard deviation of jitter and shimmer, and the variability of F_0. Figure 4.7[3] summarizes the local features calculated within one speech unit and the measurements estimated with their respective contexts of computation are indicated in Table 4.1.

---

[3]Taken from [Grop 12] with explicit permission of the author.

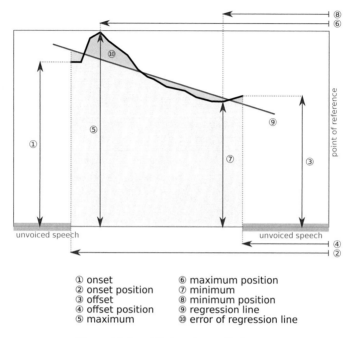

① onset   ⑥ maximum position
② onset position   ⑦ minimum
③ offset   ⑧ minimum position
④ offset position   ⑨ regression line
⑤ maximum   ⑩ error of regression line

Figure 4.7: Local F_0-based prosodic features.

4.3.2. Features based on the short-term energy

As in the case of the F_0-based features, energy-based measurements are applied to model the contour of the short-term energy of the speech units. The measurements computed with the Erlangen Prosody Module are based on speech frames of 16 ms with time shift of 10 ms.

The set of energy-based features is measured locally i.e., based on the defined contexts, (0,0) or (0,1). As in the case of the F_0-based features, this set includes the regression coefficient, the MSE of the energy contour calculated with respect to the regression curve, and the value and position of the maximum energy. Additionally, the absolute and the mean values of the energy are measured. The energy contour is normalized with respect to the mean value of the energy calculated in all of the utterance. Several measurements are estimated from the normalized contour including the regression coefficient, the MSE of the energy contour calculated with respect to the regression curve, and the values and position of the maximum and the mean energy.

Table 4.2 summarizes the energy-based measurements and their context of computation.

Feature	Context 0	Context 1
Regression coefficient	•	
	•	•
Regression error (MSE)	•	
	•	•
Maximum	•	
Minimum	•	
Mean	•	
	•	•
Onset (value and position)	•	
Offset (value and position)	•	
Jitter and shimmer periods	•	
Variance of jitter and shimmer	•	
Average jitter and shimmer	Global	
Standard deviation of jitter and shimmer	Global	
Standard deviation of F_0	Global	

Table 4.1: F_0-based features and the context of computation

Feature	Context 0	Context 1
Regression coefficient	•	
	•	•
Regression error (MSE)	•	
	•	•
Absolute energy	•	
	•	•
Maximum (value and position)	•	
Mean	•	
	•	•
Absolute normalized energy (E_n)	•	
	•	•
Regression coefficient of E_n	•	
Regression error (MSE) of E_n	•	
Maximum of E_n (value and position)	•	
Mean value of E_n	•	

Table 4.2: Energy-based features and the context of computation

4.3.3.   Features based on the duration

The duration-based features are applied to model timing in speech. In other studies this approach has been used for modeling the temporal lengthening of words [Hade 07, Stei 09, Hade 15]; however, as one of the aims of this thesis is to perform language-independent processing of speech signals, the duration-based are defined for the speech units based on the voiced/unvoiced frames, as in the previously described F_0-based and energy-based features.

The set of duration-based features includes the absolute duration length calculated over the (0,0) and (0,1) contexts, and the length of the filled pauses e.g., "uhm", "ehh", "uh", which are measured before and after the speech unit. Along with these local features, there is a set with global measurements calculated for the voiced and unvoiced frames separately. The set includes the number of voiced and unvoiced frames, their average duration, and their maximum length. The ratio between the number of voiced and unvoiced frames and the fraction of voiced and unvoiced frames are also calculated. The set of duration-based features and the computation context is summarized Table 4.3.

Feature	Context 0	1
Absolute duration length	●	
	●	●
Length of filled pauses before the unit	●	
Length of filled pauses after the unit	●	
Number of voiced and unvoiced frames	Global	
Average duration of voiced and uvoiced frames	Global	
Maximum lenght of voiced and unvoiced frames	Global	
Ratio between the number of voiced and unvoiced frames	Global	
Fraction of voiced and unvoiced frames	Global	

Table 4.3: Duration-based features and the context of computation

4.4.   Automatic classification and regression

The modeling of speech signals with different approaches has been shown in this chapter. The i-th voice register $x_i(n)$ e.g., a word, a voiced/unvoiced frame, or a short-term voice window, is represented by a set of measurements that form a d-dimensional feature vector $\mathbf{x} \in \mathbb{R}^d$ and $i = 1, 2, \ldots, M$ is the number of voice registers, which is also the number of speakers when each participant only produces one repetition of the utterance.

Two different tasks will be addressed in this Section. One consists on the design of a system able to automatically discriminate between speech recordings produced by PD patients and recordings of healthy speakers. The other task consists on develop a model to predict the neurological state of the patient according to the MDS-UPDRS-III scale. The first task is addressed in this thesis considering Support Vector Machines (SVM) and the second one considering Support Vector Regressors (SVR). These two techniques are chosen for this thesis because have shown very good performance in similar applications such as emotion recognition and voice pathology detection. The details of how these two techniques work are shown in the following Sub-sections. For a deeper understanding of the theory of support vector machines for classification and regression, it is recommended to see the book [Scho 02]

4.4.1. Hard-Margin Support Vector Machines (HM-SVM)

A support vector machine with hard margin addresses the case where the data is linearly separable i.e., it is possible to find an optimum hyperplane that perfectly separates both classes. The feature vectors $\mathbf{x}_i \in \mathbb{R}^d$ and the labels assigned to each feature vector e.g., healthy or PD, $y_i \in \{-1, +1\}$, $i = 1, 2, \ldots, M$, form the dataset $\{\mathbf{x}_i, y_i\}$. M is the number of elements of the dataset e.g, number of speakers. Note that boldface variables indicate vectors.

Let's assume that there is a hyperplane which separates elements with $y_i = +1$ from elements with $y_i = -1$. The points $\mathbf{x}_i$ that lie on the hyperplane satisfy $\langle \mathbf{w}, \mathbf{x}_i \rangle + b = 0$, where $\mathbf{w}$ is the vector normal to the hyperplane, $\frac{|b|}{||\mathbf{w}||}$ is the perpendicular distance from the origin to the hyperplane, and $||\mathbf{w}||$ is the Euclidean norm of $\mathbf{w}$. If the data is linearly separable, all the points will satisfy the constraints

$$\langle \mathbf{w}, \mathbf{x}_i \rangle + b \geq +1 \text{ for } y_i = +1 \tag{4.24}$$

and

$$\langle \mathbf{w}, \mathbf{x}_i \rangle + b \leq -1 \text{ for } y_i = -1, \tag{4.25}$$

which can be expressed in one inequality as

$$- y_i \left(\langle \mathbf{w}, \mathbf{x}_i \rangle + b \right) + 1 \leq 0, \ i = 1, 2, \ldots, M. \tag{4.26}$$

Note that the perpendicular distance from the origin to the hyperplane of the points with $y_i = +1$ is $\frac{|1-b|}{||\mathbf{w}||}$ and to the hyperplane of the points with $y_i = -1$ is $\frac{|-1-b|}{||\mathbf{w}||}$, hence the width of the margin between both hyperplanes is $\frac{2}{||\mathbf{w}||}$. Figure 4.8 illustrates the case with two-dimensional feature vectors.

The idea of the SVM is to find the pair of hyperplanes that maximize the margin. This idea can be formulated as the following optimization problem:

$$\begin{aligned} \underset{\mathbf{w}, b}{\text{minimize}} \quad & \frac{1}{2}||\mathbf{w}||^2 \\ \text{subject to} \quad & - y_i \left(\langle \mathbf{w}, \mathbf{x}_i \rangle + b \right) + 1 \leq 0, \ i = 1, 2, \ldots, M. \end{aligned} \tag{4.27}$$

Those points for which $y_i \left(\langle \mathbf{w}, \mathbf{x}_i \rangle + b \right) - 1 = 0$ holds i.e., those vectors which lie on the $\mathcal{H}_{+1}$ or $\mathcal{H}_{-1}$ hyperplanes, are called *support vectors*. In Figure 4.8 they are indicated with additional circles.

The typical way to solve this constrained convex optimization problem is introducing the Lagrangian multipliers α_i, $i = 1, 2, \ldots, M$. Then the optimization problem can be re-formulated as

$$\begin{aligned} L_P(\mathbf{w}, b, \alpha_i) &\equiv \frac{1}{2}||\mathbf{w}||^2 + \alpha_i \sum_{i=1}^{M} \left[-y_i(\langle \mathbf{w}, \mathbf{x}_i \rangle + b) + 1 \right] \\ &\equiv \frac{1}{2}||\mathbf{w}||^2 - \sum_{i=1}^{M} \alpha_i y_i (\langle \mathbf{w}, \mathbf{x}_i \rangle + b) + \sum_{i=1}^{M} \alpha_i. \end{aligned} \tag{4.28}$$

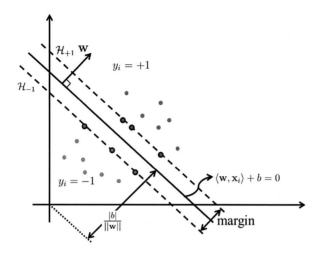

Figure 4.8: Hard-Margin Support Vector Machine.

$L_P(\mathbf{w}, b, \alpha_i)$ is the Lagrangian of the primal problem and $\alpha_i \geq 0$ $i = 1, 2, \ldots, M$ are the Lagrangian multipliers associated to the inequality constraint. The optimal conditions of the problem can be found taking the gradient in 4.28 and making it equal to zero, thus

$$\frac{\partial L_P}{\partial \mathbf{w}} = \mathbf{w} - \sum_{i=1}^{M} \alpha_i y_i \mathbf{x}_i = 0$$
$$\therefore \mathbf{w} = \sum_{i=1}^{M} \alpha_i y_i \mathbf{x}_i$$

(4.29)

and

$$\frac{\partial L_P}{\partial b} = -\sum_{i=1}^{M} \alpha_i y_i = 0$$
$$\therefore \sum_{i=1}^{M} \alpha_i y_i = 0$$

(4.30)

As the constraints of this problem are affine, according to the Slater's theorem [Slat 50], the duality gap is zero. It means that it is possible to formulate the Lagrangian dual problem L_D, and the optimal parameters in L_P will also be optimal for L_D. Additionally, the Karush-Kuhn-Tucker (KKT) conditions [Karu 39, Kuhn 51] provide the necessary and sufficient conditions for a point $\mathbf{x}^*$ to be an optimum. Such conditions are:

1. The primal constraints

$$y_i(\langle \mathbf{w}, \mathbf{x}_i \rangle + b) - 1 \geq 0, \ i = 1, 2, \ldots, M.$$

(4.31)

2. The complimentary slackness

$$\alpha_i \left[y_i(\langle \mathbf{w}, \mathbf{x}_i \rangle + b) - 1 \right] = 0, \ i = 1, 2, \ldots, M. \tag{4.32}$$

3. The dual constraints

$$\alpha_i \geq 0, \ i = 1, 2, \ldots, M. \tag{4.33}$$

4. The gradient of the Lagrangian is zero i.e., $\nabla L_P = 0$, which can be re-written as

$$\frac{\partial L_P}{\partial \mathbf{w}} = 0 \ \Rightarrow \ \mathbf{w} = \sum_{i=1}^{M} \alpha_i y_i \mathbf{x}_i, \tag{4.34}$$

and

$$\frac{\partial L_P}{\partial b} = 0 \ \Rightarrow \ \sum_{i=1}^{M} \alpha_i y_i = 0. \tag{4.35}$$

Substituting these conditions into the primal problem, the Wolfe dual [Wolf 61] is found as

$$L_D \equiv \sum_{i=1}^{M} \alpha_i - \frac{1}{2} \sum_{i=1}^{M} \sum_{j=1}^{M} \alpha_i \alpha_j y_i y_j \langle \mathbf{x}_i, \mathbf{x}_j \rangle. \tag{4.36}$$

This formulation allows finding the optimal points if the KKT conditions hold. Additionally, the complimentary slackness condition is defined as $\alpha_i \left[y_i(\langle \mathbf{w}, \mathbf{x}_i \rangle + b) - 1 \right] = 0$. It is interesting because if $\alpha_i > 0$, then $y_i(\langle \mathbf{w}, \mathbf{x}_i \rangle + b) - 1 = 0$, which means that all vectors $\mathbf{x}_i$ associated to $\alpha_i > 0$ are elements of the boundary hyperplane and comprise the set of support vectors.

Note that until this point, the perfect separability of the data has been assumed. However, this is not the case in real-world applications. In order to address the case when the data is not perfectly separable i.e., where there are errors that could be made by the machine, the support vector machines with soft margin are introduced in the next section.

4.4.2. Soft-Margin Support Vector Machines (SM-SVM)

The extension of the perfect separable case to the non-perfect separable one consists on introducing a further cost in the primal objective function to penalize the errors. This approach allows making errors in the classification, but there is a cost that has to be payed for those errors. Such cost is introduced using positive slack variables ξ_i (with $i = 1, 2, \ldots, M$) in the constraints of the optimization problem [Cort 95], such that the new set of constraints is:

$$\begin{aligned} \langle \mathbf{x}_i, \mathbf{w} \rangle + b &\geq 1 - \xi_i \text{ for } y_i = +1 \\ \langle \mathbf{x}_i, \mathbf{w} \rangle + b &\geq -1 + \xi_i \text{ for } y_i = -1 \\ \xi_i &\geq 0 \ i = 1, 2, \ldots, M. \end{aligned} \tag{4.37}$$

Note that the errors of the machine are made when $\xi_i > 1$, then $\sum_{i=1}^{M} \xi_i$ is an upper bound for the training errors. The cost of those errors are introduced in the objective function which now is defined as

$$\underset{\mathbf{w}, b, \xi_i}{\text{minimize}} \ \frac{1}{2} ||\mathbf{w}||^2 + C \left(\sum_{i=1}^{M} \xi_i \right)^k, \tag{4.38}$$

where C is an arbitrary chosen parameter such that larger C means higher penalty to the errors. Note that for any $k \in \mathbb{Z}^+$, the objective function is still convex. So, let's take $k = 1$ for simplicity and formulate the new primal Lagrangian as

$$L_P(\mathbf{w}, b, \alpha_i, \mu_i, \xi_i) = \frac{1}{2} ||\mathbf{w}||^2 + C \sum_{i=1}^{M} \xi_i - \sum_{i=1}^{M} \alpha_i \left[y_i (\langle \mathbf{x}_i, \mathbf{w} \rangle + b) - 1 + \xi_i \right] - \sum_{i=1}^{M} \mu_i \xi_i,$$
(4.39)

where μ_i are the Lagrangian multipliers introduced so that $\xi_i > 0$. The KKT conditions associated to the primal Lagrangian defined in 4.39 are:

1. The primal constraints

$$y_i (\langle \mathbf{x}_i, \mathbf{w} \rangle + b) - 1 + \xi_i \geq 0$$
(4.40)

and

$$\xi_i \geq 0,$$
(4.41)

2. The complimentary slackness

$$\alpha_i \left[y_i (\langle \mathbf{x}_i, \mathbf{w} \rangle + b) - 1 + \xi_i \right] = 0$$
(4.42)

and

$$\mu_i \xi_i = 0,$$
(4.43)

3. The dual constraints

$$\alpha_i \geq 0$$
(4.44)

and

$$\mu_i \geq 0,$$
(4.45)

4. The gradient of the Lagrangian such that $\nabla L_P = 0$ i.e.,

$$\frac{\partial L_P}{\partial \mathbf{w}} = 0 \Rightarrow \mathbf{w} - \sum_{i=1}^{M} \alpha_i y_i \mathbf{x}_i = 0$$

$$\therefore \mathbf{w} = \sum_{i=1}^{M} \alpha_i y_i \mathbf{x}_i,$$
(4.46)

$$\frac{\partial L_P}{\partial b} = 0 \Rightarrow \sum_{i=1}^{M} \alpha_i y_i = 0,$$
(4.47)

and

$$\frac{\partial L_P}{\partial \xi_i} = 0 \Rightarrow C - \alpha_i - \mu_i = 0$$
(4.48)

Note that the threshold b can be computed considering the conditions 4.43 and 4.48 for the case where $0 < \alpha_i < C$. In 4.43 at least one of the two terms has to be zero, and if $\alpha_i < C$, in 4.48 the result is $\mu_i > 0$, then $\xi_i = 0$. Thus conditioning $0 < \alpha_i < C$, the value of b can be computed from 4.42.

Replacing these results into the primal Lagrangian L_P, the Wolfe dual is found as

$$L_D \equiv \sum_{i=1}^{M} \alpha_i - \frac{1}{2} \sum_{i=1}^{M} \sum_{j=1}^{M} \alpha_i \alpha_j y_i y_j \langle \mathbf{x}_i, \mathbf{x}_j \rangle$$

subject to

$$0 \leq \alpha_i \leq C \qquad\qquad\qquad (4.49)$$

$$\sum_{i=1}^{M} \alpha_i y_i = 0.$$

Note that the border hyperplane is defined as

$$y_i \left(\langle \mathbf{x}_i, \mathbf{w} \rangle + b \right) - 1 + \xi_i = 0, \qquad\qquad (4.50)$$

and α_i has an upper bound which is defined by C. As in the case of the SVM with hard margin, the support vectors define the norm of the hyperplane i.e., $\mathbf{w} = \sum_{i=1}^{M} \alpha_i y_i \mathbf{x}_i$. The case of the SVM with soft margin is illustrated in Figure 4.9.

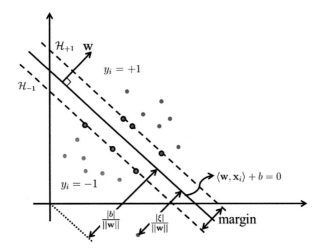

Figure 4.9: Soft-Margin Support Vector Machine.

Note that in all the previous description the existence of a linear decision function to separate the two classes in the data is assumed. The cases where such function does not exist or is not optimal need to be covered. In order to explain how the non-linear decision borders are considered, the "kernel functions" are introduced [Aize 64, Bose 92].

First, note that in all the described problems the data points appear in dot products e.g., $\langle \mathbf{x}_i, \mathbf{x}_j \rangle$. Now, the original Euclidean space where the data is described ($\mathbb{R}^d$) will be mapped to another Euclidean space $\mathbb{H}$ whose dimensionality could be infinity. The mapping function is defined as

$$\Phi : \mathbb{R}^d \longrightarrow \mathbb{H} \qquad\qquad (4.51)$$

The training process, which originally is based on dot products in the $\mathbb{R}^d$ space, now has to be done in $\mathbb{H}$ using functions like $\langle \Phi(\mathbf{x}_i), \Phi(\mathbf{x}_j) \rangle$. Assuming that there exists a kernel function such that $K(\mathbf{x}_i, \mathbf{x}_j) = \langle \Phi(\mathbf{x}_i), \Phi(\mathbf{x}_j) \rangle$ it is only necessary to define the kernel K to formulate and to solve the new optimization problem. The most common kernels used in the literature of Pattern Recognition are the polynomial and Gaussian, which are described in equations 4.52 and 4.53, respectively.

$$K(\mathbf{x}_i, \mathbf{x}_j) = (\langle \mathbf{x}_i, \mathbf{x}_j \rangle + 1)^p, \tag{4.52}$$

$$K(\mathbf{x}_i, \mathbf{x}_j) = e^{-\frac{2}{\sigma^2}||\mathbf{x}_i - \mathbf{x}_j||^2}. \tag{4.53}$$

Where p is the degree of the polynomial and σ is the bandwidth of the Gaussian kernel.

The optimization problem is the same when the kernel function is used. All the considerations made above hold when using the kernel function. Note that the norm vector $\mathbf{w}$ is still defined as $\mathbf{w} = \sum_{i=1}^M \alpha_i y_i \mathbf{x}_i$. For the case of a test data point $\mathbf{x}$, the following sign needs to be computed:

$$\text{sign}\left[f(\mathbf{x})\right] = \sum_{i=1}^{N_{sv}} \alpha_i y_i \langle \Phi(\mathbf{S}_i), \Phi(\mathbf{x}) \rangle + b = \sum_{i=1}^{N_{sv}} \alpha_i y_i K(\mathbf{S}_i, \mathbf{x}) + b, \tag{4.54}$$

where $\{\mathbf{S}_i, \ i = 1, 2, \ldots, N_{sv}\}$ is the set of support vectors.

4.4.3. Regression using support vector machines

A similar formulation can be used to address the problem of regression. In this case the model is called Support Vector Regression (SVR). In this kind of problems the labels of the data points are real-valued i.e., $y_i \in \mathbb{R}$. The analog of the soft margin SVM for regression is constructed in the space of the values $\mathbf{Y} = \{y_i\} \in \mathbb{R}$ by means of using the ε-insensitive loss function that was introduced by Vapnik [Vapn 95]. The target values are $y \in \mathbf{Y}$, and for a test point $\mathbf{x}$ the predicted function will be $f(\mathbf{x})$, thus the prediction error is determined by $|y - f(\mathbf{x})|$. As the prediction error can be above or below the target value, these two possibilities are considered using a variable that describes the margin such that $f(\mathbf{x}_i) - y_i > \varepsilon$ and $y_i - f(\mathbf{x}_i) > \varepsilon$. The loss function is illustrated in Figure 4.10.

The linear regression function can be estimated as $f(\mathbf{x}) = \langle \mathbf{w}, \mathbf{x} \rangle + b$, thus the optimization problem can be formulated as

$$\text{minimize } \frac{1}{2}||\mathbf{w}||^2 + C \sum_{i=1}^M |y_i - f(\mathbf{x}_i)|_\varepsilon, \tag{4.55}$$

where C is the penalty parameter.

Note that the expression 4.55 can be transformed into a constrained optimization problem by introducing slack variables e.g., ξ_i. Let's assign ξ when $f(\mathbf{x}_i - y_i) > \varepsilon$ and ξ^* when $y_i - f(\mathbf{x}_i) > \varepsilon$, then the primal objective function, ε-SVR can be expressed as

$$\begin{aligned} \underset{\mathbf{w} \in \mathbb{H}, \{\xi, \xi^*\} \in \mathbb{R}^M, b \in \mathbb{R}}{\text{minimize}} \quad & \frac{1}{2}||\mathbf{w}||^2 + C \sum_{i=1}^M (\xi_i + \xi_i^*) \\ \text{subject to} \quad & (\langle \mathbf{w}, \mathbf{x}_i \rangle + b) - y_i \leq \varepsilon + \xi_i, \\ & y_i - (\langle \mathbf{w}, \mathbf{x}_i \rangle + b) \leq \varepsilon + \xi_i^*, \\ & \xi_i, \ \xi_i^* \geq 0, \ i = 1, 2, \ldots, M. \end{aligned} \tag{4.56}$$

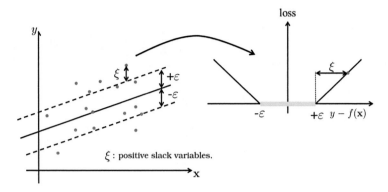

Figure 4.10: Support Vector Regressor.

The Lagrangian of this primal problem is defined as:

$$L_P \equiv \frac{1}{2}||\mathbf{w}||^2 + C\sum_{i=1}^{M}\left(\xi_i + \xi_i^*\right) - \sum_{i=1}^{M}\left(\eta_i\xi_i + \eta_i^*\xi_i^*\right) - \sum_{i=1}^{M}\alpha_i\left(\varepsilon + \xi_i + y_i - \langle\mathbf{w}, \mathbf{x}_i\rangle - b\right)$$

$$- \sum_{i=1}^{M}\alpha_i^*\left(\varepsilon + \xi_i^* - y_i + \langle\mathbf{w}, \mathbf{x}_i\rangle + b\right), \quad (4.57)$$

where $\{\alpha_i, \alpha_i^*, \eta_i, \eta_i^*\} \geq 0$. The primal variables i.e., $\mathbf{w}, b, \xi_i, \xi_i^*$, have to vanish in order to find the optimal solution such that

$$\frac{\partial L_P}{\partial \mathbf{w}} = \mathbf{w} - \sum_{i=1}^{M}\left(\alpha_i^* - \alpha_i\right)\mathbf{x}_i = 0$$

$$\therefore \ \mathbf{w} = \sum_{i=1}^{M}\left(\alpha_i^* - \alpha_i\right)\mathbf{x}_i, \quad (4.58)$$

$$\frac{\partial L_P}{\partial \xi_i} = C - \eta_i - \alpha_i = 0 \quad \text{and} \quad \frac{\partial L_P}{\partial \xi_i^*} = C - \eta_i^* - \alpha_i^* = 0$$

$$\therefore \ C = \eta_i + \alpha_i \qquad\qquad\qquad \therefore \ C = \eta_i^* + \alpha_i^*, \quad (4.59)$$

$$\frac{\partial L_P}{\partial b} = \sum_{i=1}^{M}\left(\alpha_i - \alpha_i^*\right) = 0. \quad (4.60)$$

With these results substituted into the dual optimization problem (the duality gap is zero), the result is

$$\underset{\{\alpha_i, \alpha_i^*\} \in \mathbb{R}^M}{\text{maximize}} -\frac{1}{2} \sum_{i=1}^{M} \sum_{j=1}^{M} (\alpha_i^* - \alpha_i)(\alpha_j^* - \alpha_j) \langle \mathbf{x_i}, \mathbf{x_j} \rangle - \varepsilon \sum_{i=1}^{M} (\alpha_i^* - \alpha_i) + \sum_{i=1}^{M} y_i(\alpha_i^* - \alpha_i)$$

subject to

$$\sum_{i=1}^{M} (\alpha_i^* - \alpha_i) = 0 \text{ and } 0 \leq \{\alpha_i, \alpha_i^*\} \leq C.$$

$$(4.61)$$

As $\mathbf{w} = \sum_{i=1}^{M} (\alpha_i^* - \alpha_i)\mathbf{x}_i$, the regression function can be rewritten as

$$f(\mathbf{x}) = \sum_{i=1}^{M} (\alpha_i^* - \alpha_i) \langle \mathbf{x}_i, \mathbf{x} \rangle + b \qquad (4.62)$$

Note that $\mathbf{w}$ is described by a linear combination of the training points $\mathbf{x}_i$. Additionally, as the results are based on dot products of the data, this formulation can be generalized to the kernel-based regression. Now let's verify the KKT conditions on the optimization problem.

1. The primal constraints

$$\varepsilon + \xi_i - \langle \mathbf{w}, \mathbf{x_i} \rangle - b + y_i \geq 0, \qquad (4.63)$$

$$\varepsilon + \xi_i^* - \langle \mathbf{w}, \mathbf{x_i} \rangle - b + y_i \geq 0, \text{ and} \qquad (4.64)$$

$$\{\xi_i, \xi_i^*\} \geq 0. \qquad (4.65)$$

2. The complimentary slackness

$$\alpha_i \left(\varepsilon + \xi_i - \langle \mathbf{w}, \mathbf{x_i} \rangle - b + y_i \right) = 0, \qquad (4.66)$$

$$\alpha_i^* \left(\varepsilon + \xi_i^* + \langle \mathbf{w}, \mathbf{x_i} \rangle + b - y_i \right) = 0, \qquad (4.67)$$

$$\eta_i \xi_i = 0 \text{ and } \eta_i^* \xi_i^* = 0,$$

which implies $\qquad (4.68)$

$$(C - \alpha_i)\xi_i = 0, \text{ and } (C - \alpha_i^*)\xi_i^* = 0, \text{ respectively.}$$

$$C\xi_i = 0, \text{ and } C\xi_i^* = 0 \qquad (4.69)$$

3. The dual constraints

$$0 \leq \{\alpha_i, \alpha_i^*\} \leq C, \qquad (4.70)$$

$$\sum_{i=1}^{M} (\alpha_i - \alpha_i^*) = 0. \qquad (4.71)$$

4. The gradient of the Lagrangian must be zero, which implies

$$\mathbf{w} = \sum_{i=1}^{M} (\alpha_i^* - \alpha_i)\mathbf{x}_i, \qquad (4.72)$$

$$C = \eta_i + \alpha_i \text{ and } C = \eta_i^* + \alpha_i^* \qquad (4.73)$$

Note that for $\xi_i > 0$ or $\xi_i^* > 0$, only data points $(\mathbf{x}_i, y_i)$ with corresponding $\alpha_i = C$ or $\alpha_i^* = C$ will be outside the ε-insensitive tube around $f(\mathbf{x})$. On the other hand, if $0 < \alpha_i < C$ or $0 < \alpha_i^* < C$, then η_i and η_i^* must be greater tan zero, respectively. Thus, to hold the condition in 4.69 ξ_i and ξ_i^* must be zero. Replacing into 4.66 and 4.67, the result is:

$$\begin{aligned} \alpha_i \left(\varepsilon - \langle \mathbf{w}, \mathbf{x_i} \rangle - b + y_i \right) &= 0, \\ \alpha_i^* \left(\varepsilon + \langle \mathbf{w}, \mathbf{x_i} \rangle + b - y_i \right) &= 0, \end{aligned} \tag{4.74}$$

but $\{\alpha_i, \alpha_i^*\} > 0$, thus the right side of 4.74 must be zero, then the threshold b is found as

$$b = y_i - \langle \mathbf{w}, \mathbf{x_i} \rangle + \varepsilon, \text{ for } 0 < \alpha_i < C,$$

and $\qquad\qquad\qquad\qquad\qquad\qquad\qquad\qquad\qquad\qquad\qquad\qquad$ (4.75)

$$b = y_i - \langle \mathbf{w}, \mathbf{x_i} \rangle - \varepsilon, \text{ for } 0 < \alpha_i^* < C.$$

Also, when $0 < \alpha_i < C$ or $0 < \alpha_i^* < C$, for all the points that are inside the ε-tube i.e., such that $|f(\mathbf{x} - y_i)| < \varepsilon$, the Lagrangian multipliers α_i and α_i^* vanish (to satisfy the conditions 4.66 and 4.67). Note that as $\mathbf{w} = \sum_{i=1}^{N} (\alpha_i^* - \alpha_i) \mathbf{x}_i$, those points are not necessary and conversely, the points with non-vanished α_i, α_i^* are the support vectors that are used to construct the norm vector $\mathbf{w}$. Note that in the SVM the support vectors are the samples that lie on the $\mathcal{H}_{+1}$ or $\mathcal{H}_{-1}$ hyperplanes or inside the margin, while in the ε-SVR the support vectors are the samples that lie out of the ε-tube.

Chapter 5

Experimental results

This chapter comprises most of the experiments addressed during the development of this thesis. It is divided into three main sections, the first is about automatic discrimination between people with Parkinson's disease and healthy controls, the second one is about the prediction of the neurological state of PD patients according to the MDS-UPDRS-III scale, and the third one includes the analysis of the most important results. Section 5.1 includes experiments and results obtained with each speech dimension i.e., phonation, articulation, and prosody. Additionally, the experiments are performed with speech recordings of three different languages with the databases described in Chapter 3: Spanish, German, and Czech. Results of cross-language experiments are also included in this section. Section 5.2 comprises the experiments and results of predicting the MDS-UPDRS-III label assigned to the patients during the neurological evaluation. Two different approaches for training the regression model are presented. Most of the experiments described in this chapter are published in [Oroz 13a], [Oroz 14a], [Oroz 14b], [Oroz 14c], [Oroz 15a], and [Oroz 15b].

5.1. Automatic detection of Parkinson's disease in three languages

The automatic discrimination between Parkinson's patients and healthy speakers has been addressed considering different modeling strategies. Although the wide variety of performed experiments, the focus was always on analyzing different measurements and speech tasks in the light of each speech dimension i.e., phonation, articulation, and prosody. The results obtained with each group of features are presented in the next subsections. Additionally, section 5.1.4 includes the experiments and results obtained in several cross-language experiments.

The decision for the automatic detection of PD is taken with a soft-margin support vector machine (SM-SVM) with a Gaussian kernel (see section 4.4.2 for details). For the Spanish and German data, the SVMs are trained following a 10-fold cross-validation strategy i.e., 90 % of the data is used for training the model and the remaining 10 % is used for testing it. The process is repeated several times to obtain confidence intervals of the results. For the case of Czech data, due to the reduced number of speech samples, the models are trained following a leave-one-speaker-out cross-validation. The parameters of the SVM i.e., C and σ, are optimized in a grid-search up to powers of ten with $10^{-1} < C < 10^4$ and

$10^{-1} < \sigma < 10^3$. The selection criterion was based on the accuracy obtained on test data. The folds of the experiments with German and Spanish data are randomly assembled with the constraint of the balance of age and gender. Additionally, the speaker independence is guaranteed during the training and testing stages. Thus, although the selection criterion of the SVM parameters can lead to slightly optimistic accuracy estimates, the bias effect is minimal.

The results of the binary classification i.e., PD vs HC, are presented in terms of accuracy (Acc), sensitivity (Sens), and specificity (Spec). Accuracy indicates the general performance of the system, while specificity and sensitivity indicate the capability to detect PD patients and healthy speakers, respectively. Note that both, specificity and sensitivity, are statistics that may be shown in every bi-class pattern recognition problem in order to give a more accurate idea of the performance of the system in the specific task. For instance, a system with high specificity and low sensitivity can detect people with the disease very accurately, but at the same time, a person that originally is healthy could be diagnosed as pathological.

The results are also presented using the receiver operating characteristic (ROC) curve. The horizontal axis of this curve indicates the false positive rate i.e., the rate of samples erroneously detected as pathological, and the vertical axis indicates the true positive rate i.e., the rate of samples correctly classified as pathological. The area under the ROC curve (AUC) is typically used to report the general performance of a bi-class classification system in biomedical applications. Note that AUC ranges from 0 to 1, where 1 means perfect classification. Further details of the ROC curves and different strategies to assess the performance of biomedical systems based on pattern recognition techniques can be found in [Saen 06].

5.1.1. Classification with phonation features

This speech dimension can be studied considering sustained phonations of vowels which allows the analysis of periodicity, nonlinear content, and noise content of the signals. These characteristics could be impaired in PD patients due to their problems to produce a constant and stable vibration of the vocal folds. The continuous speech signals allow analyzing also periodicity in speech signals with additional information regarding the effects of pronouncing different phonemes, syllables, and words in continuous speech.

— *Periodicity and stability:* This set of features comprises measurements of jitter, shimmer, RAP, PPQ, and APQ. Jitter and shimmer are calculated in voice frames of 40 ms length with 20 ms of time-shift, while the other measurements are estimated in voice frames of 150 ms with 75 ms of time-shift. This length assures enough consecutive pitch periods for the feature estimation. Four functionals (mean value, standard deviation, kurtosis, and skewness) are calculated from each set of features, forming a 20-dimensional feature vector per phonation ($5 \times 4 = 20$). This set of features is tested in Spanish, German, and Czech. German data only includes phonations of the vowel /a/, and Czech data have recordings of the vowel /i/. For the case of Colombian data, three repetitions of the five Spanish vowels are included. As the three repetitions are considered together in the train or test subsets, the speaker independence is assured i.e., the recordings of the same speaker are only included in the test or train subsets, but not in both. The results obtained with this set of measurements are presented in Table 5.1.

Note that the accuracies are above 85 % in most of the evaluated vowels. This result suggest that the lack control of the vocal fold vibration provides discriminant information that allows the automatic detection of PD from speech with relatively high accuracies.

		Acc %	Spec %	Sens %	AUC
German	/a/	87±17	83±32	91±16	0.89
Czech	/i/	97±12	95±22	99±7	0.97
	/a/	91±6	92±7	91±12	0.92
	/e/	81±6	85±13	77±15	0.83
Spanish	/i/	84±10	82±20	86±18	0.83
	/o/	86±9	85±12	87±15	0.90
	/u/	86±7	89±15	83±13	0.85

Table 5.1: Results obtained with stability and periodicity features.

— *Noise content:* A total of six noise measures are calculated to model the noise content that appears in sustained vowels mainly due to the incomplete closure of the vocal folds during the phonation process. In PD patients the incomplete closure appears due to their lack of control of the vocal folds, producing involuntary vibrations that inhibit their complete closure. The set of features includes HNR, CHNR, NNE, GNE, VTI, and SPI. The process to estimate these measurement is described in section 4.1.2. Frames of speech with 40 ms length and 20 ms time-shift are considered to calculate the six features. The same four functionals are calculated to form a 24-dimensional feature vector per recording ($6 \times 4 = 24$). The results obtained with this approach are shown in Table 5.2.

The results obtained with the noise measurements in sustained phonations are around 75 % in most of the cases, which confirms that there is information regarding the noise content of the signals produced by the patients. However, these accuracies are not conclusive enough to perform an accurate discrimination of people with PD and healthy controls.

		Acc %	Spec %	Sens %	AUC
German	/a/	71±7	74±18	67±15	0.69
Czech	/i/	88±32	86±36	91±30	0.87
	/a/	77±7	79±14	75±12	0.77
	/e/	75±6	72±14	77±16	0.74
Spanish	/i/	77±8	75±10	79±16	0.79
	/o/	74±8	71±9	76±14	0.75
	/u/	72±8	69±18	75±18	0.76

Table 5.2: Results obtained with noise measures.

— *Nonlinear behavior:* As it was explained in section 4.1.3, the process to produce speech has a nonlinear nature. Additionally, it is already known that the incomplete closure of vocal folds produces turbulent noise in the speech signal. These two phenomena along with others already observed in the speech production process (healthy or impaired), motivate the use of nonlinear dynamic measurements to model speech signals. The set of nonlinear features that are tested in this thesis comprises a total of eighteen measurements including D_2, LLE, LZC, H, four entropy-based measures, two features based on the recurrence and fractal-scaling analysis in embedded attractors, and eight different measurements extracted from the TEO contour. Most of the nonlinear measurements are estimated in voice frames of 55 ms length with overlap of 50 %. The only exception are the features that are based on the TEO contour, which are calculated over voice frames with 40 ms length and 20 ms time-shift. After estimating the set of measurements, the four functionals are calculated to form a 72-dimensional feature vector per recording ($18 \times 4 = 72$). The results obtained with this set of features are illustrated in Table 5.3.

		Acc %	Spec %	Sens %	AUC
German	/a/	72±11	82±17	62±29	0.77
Czech	/i/	83±38	76±44	91±30	0.80
	/a/	78±7	79±11	78±12	0.77
	/e/	76±7	84±13	68±16	0.74
Spanish	/i/	72±11	71±28	72±17	0.74
	/o/	73±8	78±20	68±21	0.72
	/u/	79±9	80±16	79±20	0.78

Table 5.3: Results obtained with nonlinear behavior features.

To summarize the results obtained with the phonation features calculated from sustained phonations, Figure 5.1 shows the ROC curves of the experiments performed with recordings of the Spanish, German, and Czech databases. Note that the highest accuracies

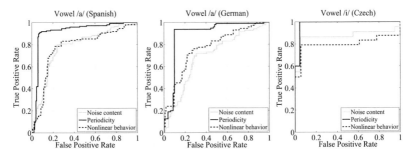

Figure 5.1: ROC curves obtained with phonation features extracted from sustained vowels.

in the three databases are obtained with periodicity measurements. This result confirms findings reported by other researchers in the literature, where the instability of the vocal fold vibration in PD patients is observed. Conversely, the results obtained with the nonlinear dynamic (NLD) features are below other results reported in the literature e.g., [Litt 09, Tsan 12]. A possible explanation for this difference is that other authors combine NLD features with other periodicity measurements such as jitter and shimmer, making difficult to conclude which measurements are actually performing the classification. Another reason for that difference in the results is that the authors do not assure the speaker independence in the experiments. This methodological problem was already discussed in section 1.2. With respect to the noise measurements, the accuracies are below 80 % except for the Czech data. This result indicates that noise features can be informative to analyze impairments in the voice of PD patients, but are not discriminant enough to perform an automatic and accurate detection of Parkinson's disease from speech.

5.1.2. Classification with articulation features

The difficulties of people with PD to control the articulators (lips, jaw, and tongue) to produce speech, can be studied recordings of sustained vowels or continuous speech signals. Several techniques to model the articulation process in different speech tasks are applied in this thesis. The details of the addressed experiments are divided into four subsections. First, the experiments performed with different spectral modeling techniques applied on sustained phonations are described. Second, different spectral-cepstral coefficients are applied to model recordings of isolated words. Third, the voiced-unvoiced modeling proposed in this thesis is tested on recordings of the isolated words, rapid repetition of the syllables /pa-ta-ka/, and isolated sentences. Finally, the voiced-unvoiced modeling and the energy content of the onset and offset transitions are applied to model read texts and monologues.

Experiments with sustained vowels

— *Spectral modeling and group delay functions:* The spectrum of the sustained phonations is modeled using eleven MFCCs, the first fourteen peaks of the high-order LPC-spectrum (LPC filter with 28 coefficients), the frequency and amplitude of the first two formants (F_1 and F_2) calculated from the MGDF-based spectrum, and the GDAM ratio. The procedure to estimate these features is described in section 4.2.2. The features are calculated in voice frames with 40 ms length and 20 ms time-shift. As in the previous experiments, the four functionals are calculated to form a 120-dimensional feature vector per recording ($30 \times 4 = 120$). The results obtained from vowels of the Spanish, German, and Czech languages are illustrated in Table 5.4. This modeling approach was published in [Bela 13] with the results obtained on a subset of recordings of the PC-GITA database.

		Acc %	Spec %	Sens %	AUC
German	/a/	66±6	62±21	70±17	0.66
Czech	/i/	91±30	95±22	86±26	0.93
	/a/	69±8	65±19	73±14	0.67
	/e/	72±9	72±19	73±14	0.72
Spanish	/i/	67±10	64±20	69±15	0.69
	/o/	75±8	73±16	78±12	0.78
	/u/	71±7	72±14	69±11	0.73

Table 5.4: Results obtained with the spectral modeling and MGDF.

Note that the results are below 70 % in most of the cases, and slightly above in only two of the Spanish vowels. The only case with higher accuracies is the Czech vowel /i/, with values of up to 91 % but with a high standard deviation. Such high variability is due to the validation strategy followed to test the models developed for these data (leave-one-speaker-out).

— Features derived from the vocal space: Additional to the exploration of the speech spectrum, the vocal space is built with the Spanish vowels. The set of features includes tVSA, the area of the vocal pentagon, and the FCR. As in the previous case, the features are calculated in voice frames with 40 ms length and 20 ms time-shift. The four functionals are calculated to form a 12-dimensional feature vector per recording ($3 \times 4 = 12$).

The accuracy obtained with this model is 65 %. This value is below the results of previous experiments and is far from other accuracies obtained with models from other speech dimensions like phonation. It perhaps indicates that longer speech units such as words, sentences, or monologues, have to be considered in order to increase the accuracy of the model. The next subsection addresses this option by means of the spectral-cepstral modeling of isolated words.

Spectral-cepstral analysis of isolated words

— Spectral-cepstral modeling: The first approach addressed in this thesis to analyze articulation in isolated words consists on spectral and cepstral modeling. This approach is applied over the recordings without separating the voiced and unvoiced segments. The main assumption is that without performing such segmentation, the information regarding co-articulatory processes is preserved.

The spectral-cepstral modeling is performed upon a set with ten isolated words of the Spanish database. Five different spectral-cepstral coefficients are applied including twelve LPCs, twelve LPCCs, twelve MFCCs, twelve PLPs, twelve RASTA-CEPS, and twenty-seven RASTA-SPEC. The process to calculate these coefficients is described in section 4.2. The four functionals are calculated on each subset of coefficients to form the corresponding feature vectors per utterance. The results are presented in Tables 5.5 and 5.6.

	LPC				LPCC				MFCC			
	Acc	Sens	Spec	AUC	Acc	Sens	Spec	AUC	Acc	Sens	Spec	AUC
gato	86	86	86	0.87	87	88	86	0.86	75	80	70	0.72
apto	84	86	82	0.81	80	82	78	0.86	77	90	64	0.77
reina	76	66	86	0.74	78	86	70	0.83	84	84	84	0.88
drama	80	92	68	0.78	90	94	86	0.90	74	78	70	0.80
grito	84	86	82	0.80	86	90	82	0.89	84	88	80	0.83
ñame	78	76	80	0.76	78	80	76	0.81	80	88	72	0.82
blusa	80	76	84	0.77	76	74	78	0.77	81	92	70	0.81
globo	85	84	86	0.86	79	84	74	0.77	73	78	68	0.70
braso	81	76	86	0.76	87	90	84	0.91	70	76	64	0.70
petaka	87	88	86	0.88	89	90	88	0.89	79	82	76	0.81

Acc, Sens, and Spec in %.

Table 5.5: Results with LPC, LPCC, and MFCC coefficients in isolated words.

The results obtained with the spectral-cepstral modeling are, in general, in the range between 70 % and 80 %. The LPCC coefficients seem to be the most appropriate to do this kind of modeling, exhibiting accuracies above 85 % in five of the ten words (*"gato, drama, grito, braso, petaka"*). In order to validate whether it is possible to improve those accuracies shown in Tables 5.5 and 5.6, the six sets of coefficients are merged in one representation space. The results of this fusion experiment are shown in Table 5.7.

	PLP				RASTA-CEPS				RASTA-SPEC			
	Acc	Sens	Spec	AUC	Acc	Sens	Spec	AUC	Acc	Sens	Spec	AUC
gato	74	86	62	0.78	83	82	84	0.82	83	78	88	0.87
apto	75	98	52	0.84	77	90	64	0.79	85	88	82	0.85
reina	83	96	70	0.88	78	82	74	0,85	81	88	74	0.85
drama	76	90	62	0.76	70	78	62	0.74	76	74	78	0.73
grito	83	80	86	0.85	81	86	76	0.83	83	78	88	0.80
ñame	79	84	74	0.82	81	84	78	0.82	85	88	82	0.90
blusa	79	70	88	0.79	75	78	72	0.78	79	86	72	0.84
globo	69	68	70	0.75	77	68	86	0.83	74	58	90	0.80
braso	78	90	66	0.82	78	80	76	0.82	79	80	78	0.85
petaka	75	84	66	0.73	80	88	72	0.81	80	88	72	0.77

Acc, Sens, and Spec in %.

Table 5.6: Results with PLP, RASTA-CEPS and RASTA-SPEC in isolated words.

Note that now the accuracies are above 80 % for nine of the ten words. Only the word *"globo"* is below but still very close (78 %). These experiments suggest that it is necessary to address a different strategy in order to increase the accuracy of the models. One alternative could be to perform the automatic segmentation of voiced and unvoiced frames to characterize them separately. The experiments addressed following this strategy are presented in the next subsection.

	Acc (%)	Sens (%)	Spec (%)	AUC
gato	87	86	88	0.90
apto	83	92	74	0.87
reina	84	92	76	0.87
drama	82	80	84	0.86
grito	85	82	88	0.86
ñame	86	90	82	0.86
blusa	83	88	78	0.85
globo	78	62	94	0.83
braso	80	84	76	0.82
petaka	81	80	82	0.82

Table 5.7: Results of merging the spectral-cepstral coefficients per word.

Voiced-Unvoiced modeling in words, syllables, and sentences

The aim of this approach is to model the processes of producing voiced and unvoiced sounds independently. The main assumption is that due to the lack of control in vocal fold vibration, PD patients are not able to stop such movement completely to produce unvoiced sounds. The motivations to state this hypothesis are the problems observed in PD patients to pronounce consonant sounds correctly, which is closely related with their lack of control of different articulators like tongue, lips, and jaw [Duff 00].

The experiments presented in this section are performed with isolated words, sentences, and the rapid repetition of the syllables /pa-ta-ka/ uttered in three languages: Spanish, Ger-

man, and Czech. The speech samples are segmented into voiced and unvoiced frames
using the software Praat [Boer 01]. Silences at the beginning and at the end of the utterances are previously removed manually. The voiced and unvoiced segments are grouped
separately. The length of each frame is verified i.e., segments shorter than 40 ms are discarded and unvoiced frames longer than 270 ms are also removed. This threshold for long
unvoiced frames was found experimentally and was equally fixed for the three databases.
As in previous approaches, speech frames of 40 ms length and 20 ms time-shift are taken.
Voiced frames are modeled considering a set with seventeen features including three noise
measures (HNR, NNE, and GNE), the first two formants (F_1 and F_2), and twelve MFCC
coefficients. For the case of the unvoiced frames, their energy content is modeled considering twelve MFCC coefficients and the energy of the signal distributed in twenty-five
Bark bands i.e., Bark band energies (BBE). The four functionals are calculated for each
set of features forming a 68-dimensional ($17 \times 4 = 68$) feature vector to model the voiced
frames and a 148-dimensional ($37 \times 4 = 148$) feature vector for the unvoiced frames of
each recording. The methodology is summarized in Figure 5.2. Where m, std, sk, and k,
represent the four functionals i.e., mean value, standard deviation, skewness, and kurtosis,
respectively. This methodology is applied on isolated words, rapid repetition of /pa-ta-

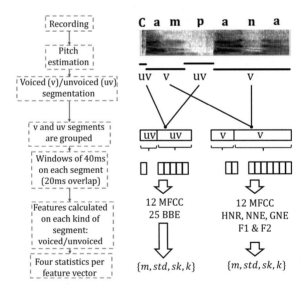

Figure 5.2: Methodology used for the voiced-unvoiced separation.

ka/, and sentences. The results obtained on each speech task spoken on each language are
described below.

— *Results with isolated words:* From the set of twenty-five Spanish words described in section 3.1.3 (Set 1), twelve were discarded because the length of their unvoiced or voiced frames was shorter than 40 ms. The results obtained with the remaining thirteen words are shown in Table 5.8. Additionally, Tables 5.9 and 5.10 include the results obtained with the German and Czech words, respectively.

		Acc %	Sens %	Spec %	AUC
gato	voiced	76±15	84±16	68±17	0.76
	unvoiced	82±6	84±15	82±20	0.83
apto	voiced	78±13	80±16	76±18	0.78
	unvoiced	81±9	86±13	77±24	0.85
campana	voiced	73±12	86±14	60±23	0.76
	unvoiced	81±12	78±28	86±16	0.81
caucho	voiced	80±16	86±14	74±25	0.83
	unvoiced	80±6	86±16	74±19	0.81
petaka	voiced	84±11	88±17	80±16	0.82
	unvoiced	79±9	78±14	82±17	0.82
coco	voiced	76±12	74±31	78±15	0.69
	unvoiced	79±8	86±25	72±19	0.77
atleta	voiced	82±9	86±14	78±20	0.79
	unvoiced	78±9	92±13	66±21	0.78
braso	voiced	75±9	86±14	64±28	0.74
	unvoiced	78±6	82±19	76±18	0.81
plato	voiced	69±6	74±19	64±23	0.64
	unvoiced	78±13	66±29	90±11	0.74
trato	voiced	77±7	90±14	64±23	0.83
	unvoiced	78±11	65±21	92±10	0.78
pato	voiced	76±8	86±14	66±17	0.75
	unvoiced	77±9	78±29	76±22	0.75
flecha	voiced	76±12	76±26	76±28	0.76
	unvoiced	77±11	88±25	66±21	0.76
presa	voiced	81±9	80±13	82±20	0.81
	unvoiced	72±6	66±28	78±22	0.66

Table 5.8: Results with voiced-unvoiced separation in Spanish words.

Note that in four of the Spanish words the accuracy obtained with the model proposed for the unvoiced frames is above 80 %. Note in Table 5.9 that with the German words the accuracies of the unvoiced features are the highest in all of the cases, ranging between 70 % and 73 %. For the case of the Czech words the accuracies are displayed in Table 5.10 and they range between 90 % and 98 %. The accuracies obtained with the features extracted from the voiced frames are between 60 % and 70 % in most of the cases, only in four words the results are above 80 %. The high accuracies of the unvoiced features in the Czech dataset can be likely explained due to the fact that the acoustic conditions of these recordings vary among speakers, thus the features are modeling the unvoiced segments of the speakers and also other phenomena like the echo and the background.

		Acc %	Sens %	Spec %	AUC
Rettungsschwimmer	voiced	69±9	59±25	79±18	0.66
	unvoiced	73±9	74±15	71±17	0.74
Bahnhofsvorsteher	voiced	72±11	67±15	78±17	0.72
	unvoiced	72±9	65±20	78±12	0.68
Toilettenpapier	voiced	71±10	69±15	73±13	0.70
	unvoiced	71±14	59±27	84±13	0.69
Bundesgerichtshof	voiced	62±8	33±17	91±10	0.65
	unvoiced	70±11	75±18	66±18	0.75
Bedienungsanleitung	voiced	68±9	65±28	69±22	0.61
	unvoiced	71±11	66±28	77±14	0.72
Perlenkettenschachtel	voiced	73±12	67±21	80±14	0.70
	unvoiced	72±5	77±13	68±9	0.71

Table 5.9: Results with voiced-unvoiced separation in German words.

		Acc %	Sens %	Spec %	AUC
pepa	voiced	87±23	73±45	99±1	0.90
	unvoiced	98±12	94±1	93±25	0.98
cukrářství	voiced	80±25	73±46	88±31	0.88
	unvoiced	97±13	99±1	94±25	0.98
sdružit	voiced	79±25	80±41	78±42	0.79
	unvoiced	97±13	99±4	93±26	0.98
tiká	voiced	79±25	84±38	74±45	0.71
	unvoiced	97±13	99±5	94±26	0.97
fouká	voiced	71±25	62±50	79±41	0.67
	unvoiced	96±13	99±1	93±25	0.97
sada	voiced	85±23	98±8	73±45	0.86
	unvoiced	96±13	99±1	93±25	0.97
kuká	voiced	77±25	77±43	78±42	0.68
	unvoiced	96±13	99±2	93±25	0.97
tři	voiced	79±25	72±46	85±37	0.74
	unvoiced	93±18	99±1	87±35	0.96
vzhůru	voiced	68±25	58±50	79±41	0.68
	unvoiced	93±17	99±3	88±34	0.91
funkční	voiced	81±25	91±29	71±47	0.86
	unvoiced	91±20	99±5	81±40	0.92
vstříc	voiced	81± 25	81±39	81±38	0.84
	unvoiced	91±20	98±4	81±40	0.90
chata	voiced	67±24	80±40	54±50	0.73
	unvoiced	90±20	99±1	81±40	0.89

Table 5.10: Results with voiced-unvoiced separation in Czech words.

Using the unvoiced features, the words with accuracies above 80 % in Spanish are: *gato, apto, campana*, and *caucho*. For German the highest accuracy is obtained with the word *Rettungsschwimmer* and the Czech words with accuracies above 95% are *pepa, cukrářství, sdružit, tiká, fouká, sada*, and *kuká*. The pronunciation of these words requires the accurate movement of at least one specific articulator to produce particular phonemes e.g., the velum in /k/ and /g/, the lips in /b/ and /p/, and the tongue in /t/. This result confirms clinical observations that suggest to pay attention to the modeling of those phonemes whose pronunciation requires the correct movement of different articulators [Loge 81].

— *Results with rapid repetition of the syllables /pa-ta-ka/:* The voiced-unvoiced modeling is also tested on recordings of the rapid repetition of the syllables /pa-ta-ka/ i.e., diadochokinetic (DDK) evaluation. The results are shown in Table 5.11. The accuracies obtained with the unvoiced features in Spanish and German are similar to those obtained with the voiced features; for the case of Czech recordings, the accuracy is of the unvoiced features is 98 %. As in the case of the isolated words, this high accuracy can be explained due to the difference in the acoustic conditions of the healthy and pathological speakers.

		Acc %	Sens %	Spec %	AUC
Spanish	voiced	80±9	90±14	70±19	0.82
	unvoiced	81±5	92±3	70±6	0.84
German	voiced	70±10	62±25	77±15	0.68
	unvoiced	71±5	67±8	75±8	0.78
Czech	voiced	81±25	79±42	83±38	0.78
	unvoiced	98±15	99±5	96±11	0.97

Table 5.11: Results with the diadochokinetic evaluation.

The results of the DDK evaluations are shown more compactly in Figure 5.3. Note that the AUC values obtained with the proposed approach are higher in the three cases. These results confirm the suitability and robustness of the voiced-unvoiced modeling for the automatic discrimination of speech of people with PD and healthy controls.

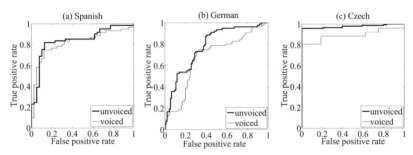

Figure 5.3: ROC curves of the DDK evaluations modeled with the voiced and unvoiced features.

— *Results with isolated sentences:* The set of six Spanish sentences considered in these experiments is described in Table 5.12. The voiced-unvoiced modeling addressed here is based on the procedure depicted in Figure 5.2. The same sets of measurements used in the isolated words to model voiced and unvoiced frames are used for the sentences.

Sentence 1:	Mi casa tiene tres cuartos.
Sentence 2:	Omar, que vive cerca, trajo miel.
Sentence 3:	Laura sube al tren que pasa.
Sentence 4:	Los libros nuevos no caben en la mesa de la oficina.
Sentence 5:	Rosita Niño, que pinta bien, donó sus cuadros ayer.
Sentence 6:	Luisa Rey compra el colchón duro que tanto le gusta.

Table 5.12: Set of Spanish sentences included in the experiments.

Table 5.13 shows the results obtained with the Spanish sentences. Note that the results obtained with the features extracted from the unvoiced segments are similar to those obtained with the features of the voiced frames. This result confirms the observations previously made with isolated words.

	Acc %	Sens %	Spec %	AUC
		Sentence 1		
voiced	74±13	84±18	64±32	0.69
unvoiced	76±9	72±23	84±16	0.83
		Sentence 2		
voiced	78±9	84±16	72±17	0.80
unvoiced	74±8	73±14	78±17	0.76
		Sentence 3		
voiced	81±12	88±14	74±19	0.83
unvoiced	80±6	82±19	78±14	0.85
		Sentence 4		
voiced	78±11	78±18	78±18	0.79
unvoiced	80±9	88±16	72±21	0.80
		Sentence 5		
voiced	77±12	80±13	74±21	0.81
Unvoiced	70±10	58±28	84±15	0.74
		Sentence 6		
voiced	79±11	84±13	74±21	0.82
unvoiced	81±7	78±19	86±13	0.81

Table 5.13: Results obtained with Spanish sentences.

Table 5.14 contains the texts of the five German sentences that the participants read during the recording sessions. Table 5.15 displays the accuracies obtained with the voiced-

Sentence 1:	Peter und Paul essen gerne Pudding.
Sentence 2:	Das Fest war sehr gut vorbereitet.
Sentence 3:	Seit seiner Hochzeit hat er sich sehr verändert.
Sentence 4:	Im Inhaltsverzeichnis stand nichts über Lindenblütentee.
Sentence 5:	Der Kerzenständer fiel gemeinsam mit der Blumenvase auf den Plattenspieler.

Table 5.14: Set of German sentences included in the experiments.

unvoiced modeling. Note that, in general, the voiced features exhibit better accuracies which indicates that maybe the unvoiced features are not the most appropriate approach to model isolated sentences in German.

	Acc %	Sens %	Spec %	AUC
	Sentence 1			
voiced	72 ± 7	72 ± 13	72 ± 10	0.70
unvoiced	66 ± 10	63 ± 18	68 ± 18	0.65
	Sentence 2			
voiced	72 ± 4	61 ± 17	83 ± 13	0.73
unvoiced	69 ± 12	63 ± 32	76 ± 14	0.69
	Sentence 3			
voiced	77 ± 10	78 ± 12	78 ± 16	0.75
unvoiced	71 ± 11	77 ± 15	67 ± 26	0.74
	Sentence 4			
voiced	73 ± 9	69 ± 13	76 ± 12	0.76
unvoiced	75 ± 10	69 ± 17	80 ± 13	0.74
	Sentence 5			
voiced	78 ± 9	81 ± 11	76 ± 16	0.77
unvoiced	71 ± 7	65 ± 17	77 ± 13	0.70

Table 5.15: Results obtained with German sentences.

The texts of the sentences pronounced by the Czech speakers are shown in Table 5.16, and the results obtained with each sentence are included in Table 5.17. Note that these sentences are actually questions that differ in a couple of words among them.

Question 1:	Kolik máte teď u sebe asi peněz?
Question 2:	Kolikpak máte teďka u sebe asi peněz?
Question 3:	Kolikpak máte teďka u sebe asi tak peněz?

Table 5.16: Set of Czech questions included in the experiments.

In most of the cases in Spanish and Czech, the highest accuracies obtained with the sentences of the three databases are obtained with the unvoiced frames. For the case of German sentences, the results are not the highest but are relatively close to those obtained with the

	Acc %	Sens %	Spec %	AUC
	Question 1			
voiced	78±25	71±46	84±37	0.79
unvoiced	97±13	99±2	94±25	0.95
	Question 2			
voiced	78±25	78±43	78±42	0.78
unvoiced	94±17	99±1	88±34	0.93
	Question 3			
voiced	82±25	94±21	69±47	0.91
unvoiced	99±2	99±1	98±2	0.99

Table 5.17: Results obtained with Czech questions.

voiced features. The proposed approach seems to be suitable to be applied in different languages and its main advantage over other approaches is that it can be directly associated to the problem of PD patients to produce strong consonants. The highest accuracies obtained in each database are: Spanish 81 % (sentence 6); German 75 % (sentence 4); and Czech 99 % (Question 3). Figure 5.4 shows these results with more detail.

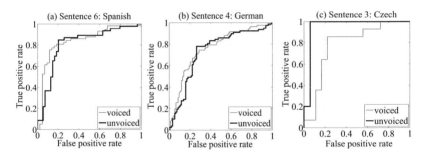

Figure 5.4: ROC curves of different sentences characterized with the voiced and unvoiced features.

In general terms, the approach proposed for modeling the energy content of the unvoiced frames exhibits higher results than the models applied on voiced segments. Further, the results obtained with some isolated words and with the DDK evaluations are higher than with the isolated sentences. The main advantage of assessing words and rapid repetition of syllables is that the medical expert can analyze more clear which articulatory movements are more impaired in the patients. However, longer utterances like isolated sentences, enable more natural assessments (closer to conversational speech), and allow also to control the sounds and articulatory movements that the medical expert wants to screen because they are still text-dependent or predefined. Thus, the three speech tasks evaluated in this subsection can be considered complimentary because enable the assessment of similar phenomena but within different contexts.

Voiced-Unvoiced and onset-offset modeling in read texts and monologues

Read texts and monologues allow assessing speech signals produced more naturally by the speakers. These tasks could show impairments that are not evident in other speech exercises like isolated words. In order to exploit the advantages of these two speech tasks in the light of the voiced and unvoiced separation, several sets of features are calculated.

— *Voiced features in Spanish read texts and monologues:* As the measurements used in this thesis so far to model voiced frames did not show important improvements when tested in isolated words and sentences, this characterization approach is changed for modeling the read texts and monologues produced by the Colombian speakers. The voiced frames are characterized considering twelve MFCCs, the variability of F_0, and the relative and absolute values of jitter and shimmer. The four functionals are calculated forming a 48-dimensional feature vector per recording ($17 \times 4 = 48$). The details of the texts that the people read are given in section 3.1.3. The results obtained with this approach are shown in Table 5.18.

	Acc %	Sens %	Spec %	AUC
read text	84 ± 10	80 ± 21	88 ± 14	0.85
monologue	81 ± 7	86 ± 17	76 ± 21	0.85

Table 5.18: Results with voiced features extracted from read texts and monologues spoken in Spanish.

The results indicated in Table 5.18 are in the same range of those obtained with the voiced features extracted from isolated sentences and words. Thus, it seems like the voiced segments do not reflect as clear as the unvoiced features, the existence of Parkinson's disease in the patients (at least with the sets of measurements that have been tested in this thesis).

— *Models for the unvoiced frames and the onset-offset transitions:* In the previous experiments, the highest accuracies are obtained by modeling the energy content of the unvoiced frames. This method will also be tested in the read texts and monologues of the three databases in order to know whether this approach is suitable for longer and more naturally spoken continuous speech signals. Further, the question regarding which phenomenon in the patients speech is being modeled by this approach will be addressed.

The hypothesis written in section 4.2.3 is formulated in order to trigger experiments that help answering such question. The motivation to raise that hypothesis came after collecting several data at *Fundalianza Parkinson Colombia* in Medellín. During these recording sessions, together with other members of the GITA[1] and SISTEMIC[2] research groups, we were collecting different signals such as speech, gait, video, and on-line writing. Having a look of the gait patterns in Parkinson's patients it can be easily evidenced that they have difficulties to start and/or to stop walking. Similar patterns can also be observed when they are writing. Thus, these patterns should be also reflected when producing speech. As the main starting/stopping processes in speech production are the vibration of vocal folds, the easiest way to model those difficulties from speech is to detect the borders between voiced and unvoiced frames i.e., onset and offset, and to calculate their energy content. In

---

[1]Grupo de Investigación en Telecomunicaciones Aplicadas
[2]Sistemas Embebidos e Inteligencia Computacional

this sense, the main difference of the methodologies for modeling unvoiced frames and the onset-offset transitions is illustrated in Figure 4.5. Like in the previous experiments, the unvoiced segments are characterized within frames of 40 ms length with 20 ms time-shift. For the onset-offset transitions, 40 ms of signal is taken to the right and to the left of the border, forming a speech chunk of 80 ms. Then, frames of 20 ms length with 10 ms time-shift are considered for the characterization process. The set of features measured upon all the segmented frames includes twelve MFCCs and twenty-five BBEs. The four functionals are calculated to form a 148-dimensional feature vector per recording ($37 \times 4 = 148$).

The results obtained with the read texts of the three databases are shown in Table 5.19. The set of features used to model the energy content of the onsets and offsets exhibit accuracies above 70 % in the three databases. With respect to the accuracy obtained with the energy of the unvoiced frames, in Czech recordings it is around 97 %, while in German and Spanish is around 74 % and 78 %, respectively. These results are shown more compactly in the ROC curves of Figure 5.5.

		Acc %	Sens %	Spec %	AUC
	unvoiced	78±3	76±6	80±4	0.81
Spanish	onset	82±2	90±5	76±7	0.84
	offset	80±9	82±22	78±9	0.79
	unvoiced	74±4	84±5	64±7	0.78
German	onset	80±6	79±9	82±9	0.80
	offset	79±3	73±2	85±6	0.79
	unvoiced	97±12	99±15	99±26	0.95
Czech	onset	94±21	99±17	88±27	0.93
	offset	93±25	99±21	85±12	0.88

Table 5.19: Results obtained with the features of the unvoiced frames and the onset-offset transitions extracted from read texts.

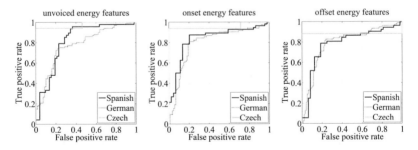

Figure 5.5: ROC curves obtained with the features of the unvoiced frames and the onset-offset transitions extracted from the read texts.

The results of the experiments performed with the recordings of the monologues are shown in Table 5.20. The accuracies obtained with these recordings are mostly around 80 %. These results confirm the presence of highly discriminant information in the onset-offset transitions which are closely related with the processes of starting-stopping the vocal fold vibration. Note that the accuracies obtained with the monologues are higher than those obtained with the read texts, which can be likely explained due to the richness of the monologues in terms of variety of words, syllables, and articulatory movements. Another possible explanation can be because the motor-planning process in spontaneous speech is more complex, which contributes to make more articulation errors and disfluency in patients with PD.

		Acc %	Sens %	Spec %	AUC
	unvoiced	71±5	56±16	89±16	0.75
Spanish	onset	83±3	84±8	80±8	0.83
	offset	76±7	92±9	62±9	0.78
	unvoiced	80±3	73±8	86±2	0.80
German	onset	73±5	72±9	73±39	0.75
	offset	81±2	75±6	87±9	0.79
	unvoiced	98±15	98±21	99±16	0.99
Czech	onset	99±26	99±27	99±17	0.99
	offset	93±29	85±21	99±22	0.96

Table 5.20: Results obtained with the features of the unvoiced frames and the onset-offset transitions extracted from monologues.

The performance of the three characterization methods i.e., energy content of the unvoiced frames, and of the onset-offset transitions, is shown more compactly in the ROC curves of Figure 5.6.

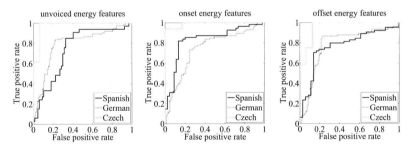

Figure 5.6: ROC curves obtained with the features of the unvoiced frames and the onset-offset transitions extracted from monologues.

The suitability and robustness of the methods proposed in this thesis to discriminate between speech of people with PD and healthy controls is confirmed in both, read texts and monologues. Additionally, the simplicity of this approach enable other researchers to reproduce it. For instance, a group of researchers from *Telefónica I+D*[3] in Barcelona (Spain) worked with the PC-GITA database and reproduced the methods and results described in this thesis.

---

[3]http://www.tid.es/
Last retrieved 7/2/2015.

5.1.3. Classification with prosody features

Prosody features are used for modeling timing and intonation in continuous speech. A subset of sixty four features of the prosody module developed by the Chair of Pattern Recognition at the Friedrich-Alexander-Universiät Erlangen-Nürnberg is used in this thesis to model prosodic characteristics of Parkinson's speech (see section 5.1.3 for further details of the features). The prosodic features are used in this thesis to model isolated sentences, read texts, and monologues spoken in Spanish, German, and Czech. The results obtained with each speech task are described in the next subsections.

Prosodic modeling in isolated sentences

The prosodic features are tested on the sets of sentences pronounced by the speakers of the three languages. As in the previous experiments, four functionals are calculated from each measurement, forming a 256-dimensional feature vector per recording ($64 \times 4 = 256$). The results obtained with the sets of sentences of Spanish, German, and Czech are shown in Tables 5.21, 5.22, and 5.23, respectively. The order of the sentences is the same as in the previous experiments.

Sentence #	Acc %	Sens %	Spec %	AUC
1	81±10	88±17	74±27	0.81
2	76±11	80±23	72±17	0.78
3	84±13	84±26	84±16	0.83
4	73±8	88±14	58±22	0.73
5	78±8	94±14	62±22	0.87
6	77±13	86±10	68±25	0.82

Table 5.21: Results with the prosody features in Spanish sentences.

Sentence #	Acc %	Sens %	Spec %	AUC
1	73±12	74±16	71±17	0.71
2	76±8	77±15	75±12	0.76
3	82±6	86±11	77±13	0.84
4	80±6	79±19	81±15	0.79
5	81±8	78±12	84±9	0.81

Table 5.22: Results with the prosody features in German sentences.

Question #	Acc %	Sens %	Spec %	AUC
1	72±24	52±51	92±24	0.79
2	90±20	84±37	95±18	0.89
3	94±16	94±25	95±20	0.93

Table 5.23: Results with the prosody features in Czech sentences.

The accuracies obtained with the subset of features of the Erlangen prosody module range between 72 % and 94 %, which indicates that there is information in the prosodic structure of the patients speech that could complement the information provided by other dimensions like articulation. Additionally, note that the accuracies obtained in the second and third questions of the Czech data are higher than those obtained with the other approaches like the voiced and unvoiced modeling. It seems that the prosodic features are capturing information regarding differences in the way that PD patients intonate questions. Unfortunately, these are the only questions included in the datasets considered in this thesis, so was not possible to do further experiments with questions pronounced in the other languages to verify this hypothesis.

Prosodic modeling in read texts and monologues

The same set of prosodic features used in the sentences is used for modeling the read texts and monologues of the three languages, then the four functionals are calculated for each measurement to form a 256-dimensional feature vector per recording. The results are shown in Table 5.24 and summarized in the ROC curves of Figure 5.7.

Language	Recording	Acc %	Sens %	Spec %	AUC
Spanish	read text	68±22	77±13	86±10	0.79
	monologue	74±19	72±13	70±24	0.76
German	read text	91±7	84±8	77±12	0.83
	monologue	88±15	80±9	71±16	0.80
Czech	read text	75±44	79±25	83±39	0.76
	monologue	89±21	93±27	86±36	0.91

Table 5.24: Results with prosody features extracted from read texts and monologues spoken in Spanish, German, and Czech.

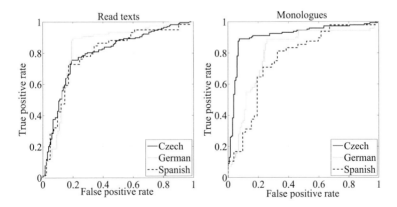

Figure 5.7: ROC curves of read texts and monologues modeled with prosodic features.

The results obtained with the prosody module in read texts and monologue are similar to those obtained with sentences of the three languages. This result suggests that in order to improve the performance of the prosodic modeling it is necessary to include features from other speech dimensions e.g., articulation. Also, it seems that the speech units defined in this thesis to compute the prosodic features i.e., the voiced segments, are not suitable to obtain high accuracies in Parkinson's disease detection. Perhaps if those units would be defined in terms of words, syllables, or phonemes, the results could increase; however, the definition of this kind of speech units requires the use of an automatic speech recognition (ASR) system, which is possible but would limit the application of the method to only those languages for which the ASR is available. As one of the aims of this thesis is to analyze and to propose different characterization methods without any assumption regarding the language spoken by the speaker, these other language-dependent speech units were not explored.

Besides the binary classification experiments (PD vs HC) introduced in the previous sections, several cross-language experiments are performed to test the generalization capability of the proposed approaches.

5.1.4. Cross-language experiments

Read texts, monologues, and the DDK evaluations of the three databases are considered for these experiments. Due to differences in the sampling frequencies of the three datasets, the recordings were re-sampled down to 16 kHz. Additionally, the cepstral mean subtraction process is applied in order to normalize the channel and avoid possible bias introduced by differences of microphones, cables, and sound cards among the databases. The experiments consist on training the SVM with samples of one language and test it on samples of another one. Additionally, some of the recordings of the language that is going to be tested are included in the training set incrementally from 10 % to 80 % of the recordings. The recordings that are added to the training set are excluded from the test set. Parts (a), (b), and (c) in Figures 5.8 and 5.9 show the improvements of the accuracies obtained with read texts and monologues, respectively, when portions of the Spanish, German, or Czech, data are included in the test sets (horizontal axis). Note that the accuracy of the system increases from around 60 % to 90 % depending on the task, the added fraction of the target language, and on the training set.

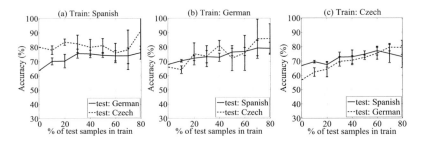

Figure 5.8: Results of cross-language experiments with read texts.

Similarly, Figure 5.10 shows the results of the cross-language experiments performed with recordings of the rapid repetition of /pa-ta-ka/. This experiment is interesting for

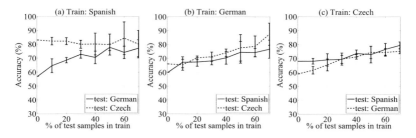

Figure 5.9: Results of cross-language experiments with the monologues.

several reasons: firstly, the DDK evaluation is one of the most commons speech tasks used to assess Parkinson's speech, and secondly, the pronunciation of the syllables /pa-ta-ka/ should not varies very much among different languages, thus the result of this experiment should show higher accuracies than in the previous cases (read texts and monologues), which depend more on each language.

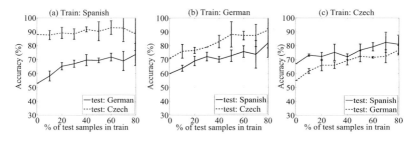

Figure 5.10: Results of cross-language experiments with the DDK evaluation.

According to the results in read texts and monologues (Figures 5.8 and 5.9, respectively), it is better to train with Czech samples when the test set is composed by German recordings. This is also true in the other way around, i.e., in general, when the test set is Czech, better results are obtained training with German samples. When the test set is Spanish the results obtained training with German and Czech are similar.

The best results obtained with the DDK evaluations (Figure 5.10) are obtained when the Czech samples are used for test. When the training set is Spanish and the test set is Czech, the behavior of the system is relatively stable with accuracies around 90 % independent on the amount of test samples included in the training set. Conversely, when Czech samples are used for training, at least 60 % of the test samples need to be added to reach accuracies of around 80 %. When the test set is German, the results of training with Spanish or Czech are similar and about 60 % of the test samples need to be added in training to reach 70 % of accuracy.

5.2. Prediction of the neurological state of Parkinson's patients

The automatic discrimination of patients with Parkinson's disease and healthy speakers is relevant because it is a step forward the development of computer aided tools that support the medical experts in the diagnosis process. However, once the patients are already diagnosed, it is necessary to monitor their neurological state and that cannot be made with the binary classification approach. An accurate monitoring of PD patients could allow making timely decisions regarding their medication and their therapy. Additionally, if such screening is performed from speech recordings, their treatment could be followed remotely, then the costs of the treatment would decrease dramatically.

In order to contribute in the development of computational systems for the assessment of the neurological state of Parkinson's patients, this thesis addresses the problem of predicting the progress of the disease using only speech signals as prior knowledge of the patients. The task consists on predict the value of the MDS-UPDRS-III scale that was assigned to each patient by the neurologist during the medical examination. As it was already highlighted in section 2.3.1, the MDS-UPDRS-III evaluates the speech of the patient in only one of the 33 items of the motor scale, making the prediction task more challenging. This scale is chosen as the reference to evaluate the prediction of the neurological state of the patients because it is considered the world-standard for the assessment of Parkinson's disease. The main assumption is that there is a strong correlation between the speech impairments of the patients and the scale.

This section is divided into two main parts. The first one considers experiments performed following a 10-fold cross-validation strategy with the fifty patients of the PC-GITA database (Colombian speakers) to train and test the regression model. The second part considers the division of the data that was performed for the organization of the *Computational Paralinguistics Challenge (ComParE)* as a special session of the conference INTERSPEECH 2015. For the challenge, an additional group of eleven patients that were recorded with different acoustic conditions is considered as the test set. The details of these experiments are given in the following subsections.

5.2.1. Regression with 10-fold cross-validation

The experiments performed following the 10-fold cross-validation strategy consider recordings of sustained phonations of the Spanish vowels and also continuous speech signals (read texts and monologues). The train and test groups are formed randomly. As there is a total of fifty patients in the database, the test sets of each fold contain recordings from five speakers. Each test set is formed with at least two patients of the same sex. The age-difference among the speakers in each fold does not exceed ten years. The regression task is addressed with an ε-SVR with linear kernel. This model is used for two reasons, (1) because it is known to be robust against overfitting, and (2) because it was the model used to calculate the baseline of the ComParE 2015, thus using the same regression model it is possible to raise more clear conclusions regarding the extracted features, which is one of the main aims of this thesis. The parameters of the regressor i.e., ε and C, are optimized in a grid-search with $C \in [10^{-4}, 10^{-3}, \ldots, 10^4]$ and $\varepsilon \in [1, 5, 10, \ldots, 50]$. The selection criterion was based on the result obtained on test data, which can lead to optimistic correlation estimates. The performance of the systems is evaluated with the Pearson's (r) and Spearman's (ρ) correlations. The highest correlation obtained on each fold is taken and then the ten values are averaged to obtain the average correlation of the given model. Spearman's correlation is included because it does not assumes any linear dependence among the features, thus it is a more realistic and conservative estimate of the prediction capability of the models. Pearson's correlation is also included because it allows analyzing possible linear relations among the estimated features. Different sets of features are extracted from the sustained vowels and from the continuous speech signals. The results obtained with each speech task are described below.

Results with sustained vowels

The sustained vowels are modeled considering different phonation and articulation features separately. The phonation modeling comprises the three groups of measurements that are used in the experiments described in section 5.1.1 and addressed with sustained vowels. The groups are summarized in the following list:

- Noise content: HNR, CHNR, NNE, GNE, VTI, and SPI.

- Periodicity: Jitter, shimmer, RAP, PPQ, and APQ.

- Nonlinear behavior: D_2, LLE, LZC, H, four entropy-based measures, two features based on the recurrence and fractal-scaling analysis in embedded attractors, and eight measurements extracted from the TEO contour.

The results obtained with the phonation features extracted from each vowel are summarized in Table 5.25. The highest correlations (Spearman's and Pearson's) are obtained with the nonlinear features. Note that these results differs from those obtained in the binary classification problem, where the highest accuracies were obtained with the periodicity measurements. This difference clearly indicates that those features that are suitable to discriminate between people with PD and healthy speakers are not necessarily suitable to predict the neurological state of the patients.

	Noise		Periodicity		Nonlinear	
	ρ	r	ρ	r	ρ	r
/a/	0.49	0.46	0.45	0.46	0.61	0.63
/e/	0.40	0.29	0.50	0.44	0.64	0.62
/i/	0.52	0.40	0.42	0.43	0.66	0.63
/o/	0.61	0.55	0.46	0.38	0.62	0.58
/u/	0.52	0.46	0.44	0.49	0.65	0.60

Table 5.25: Regression results obtained with different subsets of phonation features extracted from sustained vowels.

Experiments with two sets of articulation features are performed, one set includes those measurements derived from the vocal space i.e., tVSA, FCR, and VPA, and the other one includes the features extracted to model the voice-spectrum i.e., eleven MFCCs, the first fourteen peaks of the high-order LPC-spectrum, frequency and amplitude of F_1 and F_2 calculated from the MGDF-based spectrum, and the GDAM ratio.

The results obtained with the articulation features are summarized in Table 5.26. The last row of the table corresponds to the results obtained with the features extracted from the vocal space, thus it does not corresponds to an individual vowel. As in the case of phonation features, the highest correlation values are obtained with vowel /i/. This result indicates that this vowel is more suitable than the others to predict the neurological state of PD patients. This result is interesting because other studies in the state-of-the-art [Tsan 10a, Tsan 11] only have considered experiments with phonations of the vowel /a/, but do not include results with different vowels.

	ρ	r
/a/	0.49	0.49
/e/	0.57	0.54
/i/	0.65	0.60
/o/	0.44	0.41
/u/	0.46	0.47
tVSA, FCR, VPA	0.50	0.41

Table 5.26: Regression results obtained with different articulation features extracted from sustained vowels.

The results obtained with sustained phonations are interesting and promising; however, as it was already pointed out in previous sections, this task is limited and does not allows the evaluation of different phenomena that appear during the production of continuous speech e.g., movement of articulators, intonation, timing, and changes in energy, among others. The next subsection covers this scenario considering recordings of read texts and monologues produced by the same speakers considered in this subsection.

Results with continuous speech signals: read texts and monologues

The evaluation of continuous speech signals includes features of the three speech dimensions studied in this thesis: phonation, articulation, and prosody. As in the experiments of binary classification showed in section 5.1.2, the voiced and unvoiced segments of speech are separated and modeled independently. The sets of features used in these experiments are the same as those used in section 5.1.2, for phonation and articulation, and in section 5.1.3 for prosody. The sets of features are summarized in the following list.

- Phonation: twelve MFCCs, jitter, shimmer, and the variability of F_0.

- Articulation: twenty-five BBEs and twelve MFCCs extracted to model the energy content of the unvoiced frames, and the onset-offset transitions.

- Prosody: Sixty-four features from the Erlangen prosody module. The speech units defined for the extraction of the features are the voiced segments.

The results obtained with the three feature sets are shown in Table 5.27. The highest correlations in the experiments with the monologues are obtained with the features of the Erlangen prosody module. These are the highest correlations obtained in all of the regression experiments with 10-fold cross-validation performed in this thesis. When the features from the three dimensions are merged (last column of the table) the values of the correlations decrease in some decimals. Regarding the results with the read texts, the highest correlations are obtained with the articulation features. When the three dimensions are combined, the correlations decrease in up to three points. An additional experiment was performed combining the features from the read texts and monologues in the same representation space i.e., fusion at speaker level. The results with phonation and prosody features are similar to those obtained when the three dimensions are combined.

	Phonation		Articulation		Prosody		Fusion	
	ρ	r	ρ	r	ρ	r	ρ	r
Monologues	0.55	0.60	0.71	0.72	0.80	0.79	0.76	0.74
Read texts	0.68	0.70	0.72	0.71	0.50	0.45	0.68	0.72
Monologues & read texts	0.64	0.64	0.73	0.72	0.63	0.56	0.73	0.74

Table 5.27: Regression results obtained with phonation, articulation, and prosody features extracted from read texts and monologues.

Contrary to what was expected at the beginning of the regression experiments, the articulation features, i.e., energy of unvoiced segments and onset-offset transitions, do not exhibit the highest correlations. This result could indicate that the proposed modeling needs to be complemented with other approaches to predict the neurological state of PD patients accurately.

Since the ε-SVR parameters were optimized on test, these results can be considered as the upper bound of the performance that can be obtained with the methodology proposed in this thesis. It means that these results are, in most of the cases, highly optimistic. Although the results are relevant because allow comparing different speech tasks and different characterization strategies, in order to find more conclusive results regarding the development of computer aided tools for the monitoring of PD patients, the methodology has to be tested in more realistic conditions. The ideal scenario to do such tests is the Computational Paralinguistics Challenge (ComParE) that is organized yearly since 2009 as one of the special sessions of the International Conference of the Speech Communication Association (INTERSPEECH). The next subsection provides the details of the organization of the data and the experiments performed to address the Challenge.

5.2.2. Regression with the data of the Computational Paralinguistics Challenge (ComParE)

The challenge consists on estimating/predicting the neurological state of Parkinson's patients according to the MDS-UPDRS-III scale, within a regression task. The data used for the challenge is divided into three subsets: training, development (devel.), and test. The first two subsets are from the PC-GITA database; recordings of thirty-five patients are included in the training subset and the remaining fifteen are considered for development. The subset for test is formed with recordings from eleven additional patients (6 male and 5 female) that were recruited also in *Fundalianza Parkinson Colombia*. The speech tasks recorded from the additional group of patients are the same as those recorded in the PC-GITA database. All the 42 speech tasks described in section 3.1.3 were considered in the challenge i.e., 24 isolated words, 10 sentences, one read text, one monologue, and the rapid repetition of the syllables /pa/, /ta/, /ka/, /pa-ta-ka/, /pa-ka-ta/, and /pe-ta-ka/. The recordings of the test set were captured with the same microphone, sound card, resolution bits, and sampling frequency as in the PC-GITA database, but they were not recorded in the same acoustic conditions. The test patients were recorded in a quiet room but not in a sound-proof booth. The total duration of the recordings included in the training, development, and test sets are 81, 33, and 43 minutes, respectively. The additional group of patients were diagnosed and labeled by the same neurologist that labeled the patients of the PC-GITA database. The test speakers were recorded in ON-state as it was for the patients of PC-GITA. Details of the test patients data are provided in Table 5.28.

	AGE	UPDRS	H&Y	t (years)
	67	58	3	5
	70	64	3	3
	61	82	3	10
	71	27	1	0.5
	61	36	2	1.5
	62	20	2	6
	53	31	2	1
	65	46	3	5
	70	40	3	7
	66	12	2	8
	48	13	2	15
average	63	39	2.4	6.7

t: Time post PD diagnosis.

Table 5.28: Age, MDS-UPDRS-III, H&Y and time after PD diagnosis of the patients included in the test set of the INTERSPEECH 2015 Challenge.

Challenge baseline

The baseline of the challenge was defined considering features extracted from the 42 speech tasks using the 2.1. public release of the Munich open Speech and Music Interpretation by Large Space (OpenSMILE) [Eybe 13]. The feature set contains 6373 static features as functionals of low-level descriptor contours. An ε-SVR with linear kernel is used for the regression model. The parameters of the regressor i.e., C and ε, are optimized on the development subset. After several experiments performed by the organizers of the challenge, it was concluded that the optimal value of ε for this task is 1, thus the parameter was fixed in this value. Regarding C it was optimized on development up to powers of ten with $10^{-5} < C < 10^{-2}$. The same search-grid was used on the test set in oder to check whether the selected parameter on development is also the optimal on test. The result of this checking was that the parameter changes, the optimal value in 'train vs development' is $C = 10^{-3}$, but in 'train vs test' is $C = 10^{-5}$. The evaluation criterion was the Spearman's correlation coefficient (ρ) mainly because it is a more 'conservative' and robust estimate than the Pearson's correlation coefficient. These results are shown in Table 5.29.

	Spearman's correlations (ρ)			
	$C = 10^{-5}$	$C = 10^{-4}$	$C = 10^{-3}$	$C = 10^{-2}$
train vs devel.	0.37	0.47	0.49	0.49
train vs test	0.39	0.30	0.24	0.24

Table 5.29: Baselines of the ComParE 2015.

Experiments with phonation, articulation, and prosody features

The same distribution of the data that was used for the challenge is tested in these experiments. The aim is to analyze the suitability of each speech dimension (phonation, articulation, and prosody) to estimate/predict the neurological state of Parkinson's patients in more realistic conditions. In section 5.2.1 the experiments were performed only considering speech recordings captured in noise-controlled conditions i.e., in a sound-proof booth. Additionally, a 10-fold cross validation strategy was addressed and the parameters of the ε-SVR were optimized on the test set. These two aspects make the conditions of those experiments non-realistic and non conclusive if the aim is to develop computer aided tools for the automatic assessment/monitoring of people with Parkinson's disease. In order to validate the suitability of the measurements studied and proposed in this thesis in realistic conditions, the distribution of the data used for the organization of the ComParE challenge is considered. Unlike the experiments with 10-fold cross validation, the parameters of the ε-SVR (C and ε) are optimized on development. The samples of the test set never participate in the 'training vs development' process. The experiments addressed here only include recordings of the monologues and read texts. Values of the Spearman's and Pearson's correlations are considered and are evaluated independently during the optimization process.

The sets of features considered to model each speech dimension are the same as in section 5.2.1. The results of the Spearman's and Pearson's correlations, along with the values of the parameters optimized on development are shown in Tables 5.30 and 5.31, respectively.

		Phonation	Articulation	Prosody	Fusion
Monologues		$C = 10^{-2}; \varepsilon = 15$	$C = 1; \varepsilon = 5$	$C = 1; \varepsilon = 5$	$C = 10^{-2}; \varepsilon = 10$
	train/dev.	0.43	0.60	0.31	0.31
	train/test	0.32	0.39	-0.16	0.29
Read texts		$C = 10^{-4}; \varepsilon = 5$	$C = 10^{-2}; \varepsilon = 5$	$C = 10^{-4}; \varepsilon = 10$	$C = 10^{-4}; \varepsilon = 1$
	train/dev.	0.46	0.28	0.27	0.07
	train/test	0.5	0.33	0.1	0.43
Monologues		$C = 10^{-2}; \varepsilon = 5$	$C = 10^{-2}; \varepsilon = 5$	$C = 10^{-2}; \varepsilon = 1$	$C = 10^{-2}; \varepsilon = 10$
& read texts	train/dev.	0.51	0.28	0.04	0.22
	train/test	0.36	0.33	-0.31	0.35

Table 5.30: Spearman's correlations (ρ) obtained with monologues and read texts.

The highest Spearman's correlation is obtained with the phonation features ($\rho = 0.5$). This result is important not only because it exceeds the baseline of the challenge ($\rho = 0.39$), but also because it is obtained only with phonation features. This result allows concluding that, at least with the models and experiments considered in this thesis, the phonation impairments reflect the neurological state of PD patients better than other speech dimen-

		Phonation	Articulation	Prosody	Fusion
		$C = 10^{-4}; \varepsilon = 10$	$C = 10^{-2}; \varepsilon = 25$	$C = 1; \varepsilon = 25$	$C = 10^{-3}; \varepsilon = 1$
Monologues	train/dev.	0.58	0.43	0.33	0.32
	train/test	0.36	0.63	-0.22	0.32
		$C = 10^{-4}; \varepsilon = 5$	$C = 10^{-2}; \varepsilon = 1$	$C = 10^{-2}; \varepsilon = 1$	$C = 10^{-4}; \varepsilon = 30$
Read texts	train/dev.	0.54	0.23	0.19	0.03
	train/test	0.63	0.52	0.24	0.20
		$C = 10^{-4}; \varepsilon = 10$	$C = 10^{-2}; \varepsilon = 1$	$C = 10^{-2}; \varepsilon = 1$	$C = 10^{-4}; \varepsilon = 1$
Monologues	train/dev.	0.60	0.23	-0.1	0.09
& read texts	train/test	0.50	0.53	-0.37	0.40

Table 5.31: Pearson's correlations (r) obtained with monologues and read texts.

sions like articulation and prosody. Regarding the results with the articulation features, the highest Spearman's correlation is obtained with monologues ($\rho = 0.39$). This result equals the baseline of the challenge and enables concluding that the articulation features are the second most suitable (out of three) to estimate the neurological state of the patients. The most surprising result is obtained with the Erlangen Prosody module, which only exhibited positive correlations in test with the read texts ($\rho = 0.24$). These results can be explained due to the changes in the noise conditions of the test recordings. Additionally, as it was concluded in the binary classification experiments, it seems that the speech unit defined in this thesis to compute the prosodic features is not appropriate. On the other hand, two fusion schemes are also tested in this regression task: combining the features extracted from the monologues with those from the read texts, and combining each feature set (phonation, articulation, and prosody) extracted from each speech task. The results obtained with these fusion approaches do not show great improvements with respect to the results obtained individually, which indicates that for the task of estimating the neurological state of PD patients, the speech tasks and the feature sets are informative but not complimentary. A similar analysis can be made with the results obtained in terms of the Pearson's correlation (r). The main difference is that this coefficient assumes a linear relationship among the features, which is not true and could lead to optimistic conclusions.

The scatter-plots obtained with the articulation and phonation features extracted from the monologues and read texts, respectively, are shown in Figure 5.11. Although the variability of the original labels is higher than in the predicted ones, there is a correlation between these two data that can be observed from this figure.

Figure 5.12 shows the plots with the original and the predicted MDS-UPDRS-III labels for each patient of the test set. The upper part of the figure shows the result obtained with the articulation features extracted from the monologues, and the lower part shows the result obtained with the phonation features extracted from the read texts.

From Figure 5.12 can be estated that the patients that have the less accurate prediction in both experiments are the 2nd, 6th, 10th, and 11th. The recordings of these patients were carefully listened in order to verify whether the perceptual evaluation matches with the neurological assessment. It seems like the values in the MDS-UPDRS-III scale assigned to those patients do not reflect accurately their speech impairments. For instance, the speech of the 2nd speaker does not looks very impaired, however, this patient has a MDS-UPDRS-III value of 64. Conversely, the 10th speaker has a MDS-UPDRS-III value of 12, but his speech exhibits several articulation problems. As in the study reported by Skodda et al.,

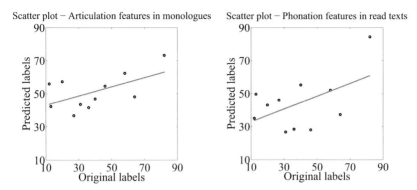

Figure 5.11: Scatter plots obtained with articulation and phonation features used to model the monologues and read texts of the ComParE 2015 test set.

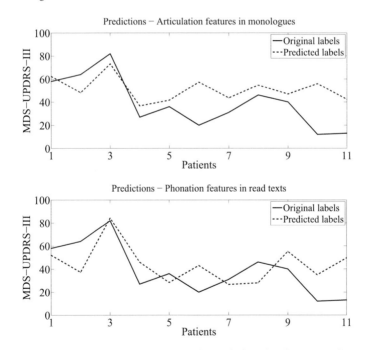

Figure 5.12: Predictions obtained with articulation and phonation features used to model the monologues and read texts of the ComParE 2015 test set.

[Skod 12], it seems like the speech impairments are the result of an escalation of axial dysfunction that is too subtle to be mirrored by the MDS-UPDRS-III scale.

Further to the experiments with phonation, articulation, and prosody features, the measurements that are proposed in this thesis to model articulation are tested independently. These experiments are designed with the aim of state which of the proposed features are more suitable to predict the neurological state of the patients. Recordings of the monologues and read texts are tested individually. The results for the Spearman's correlations are shown in Table 5.32. Note that the features from the onset transitions exhibit the highest correlations in both, monologues and read texts. The features of unvoiced and offset transitions do not show to be suitable for this task. Note that only with the features extracted from the onset transitions the baseline of the challenge is paired. It suggests that the difficulty to start the vibration of the vocal folds is the feature that reflects more accurately (among the articulation measurements tested in this thesis) the neurological state of the patients.

		unvoiced $C = 10; \varepsilon = 25$	onset $C = 1; \varepsilon = 1$	offset $C = 10^{-2}; \varepsilon = 1$
Monologues	train/dev.	0.51	0.42	0.62
	train/test	-0.23	0.39	0.08
		$C = 10^{-4}; \varepsilon = 20$	$C = 10^{-4}; \varepsilon = 10$	$C = 10^{-2}; \varepsilon = 25$
Read texts	train/dev.	0.26	0.48	0.23
	train/test	0.19	0.22	-0.24

Table 5.32: Spearman's correlations (ρ) with the articulation features.

5.3.   Analysis of the experimental results

Three speech phenomena have been studied in the experiments presented in this chapter considering recordings of three languages (Spanish, German, and Czech) and different speech tasks including sustained vowels, isolated words, repetition of syllables, sentences, read texts, and monologues. Binary classification experiments i.e., PD vs HC, are addressed in order to test the suitability of each speech task and each speech dimension (phonation, articulation, and prosody) for the automatic detection of the disease. Additionally, regression experiments with the continuous speech signals (read texts and monologues) spoken in Spanish are performed in order to assess the suitability of each speech dimension for the estimation of the neurological state of Parkinson's patients.

Sustained vowels are evaluated with several phonation and articulation measurements. According to the results, the features related with the periodicity of the signals are the most suitable to perform the automatic discrimination of PD vs HC, with accuracies around 85 % obtained with recordings from the three languages. These results are shown in Table 5.1. Regarding the isolated words, several spectral-cepstral coefficients are calculated to model articulation in those recordings. According to the results, the combination of those coefficients into one representation space seems to be less discriminant than the sustained vowels, with accuracies around 80 % in most of the cases (only Spanish words were tested with this approach). The first two formants (F_1 and F_2) were also estimated in order to model articulation from vowels and the results were around 70 %. F_1 and F_2 along with several noise measures are also used to assess isolated words and the results obtained in the three languages ranged between 70 % and 80 % in most of the cases (see Tables 5.8, 5.9, and 5.10). Further to the aforementioned methods to model articulation in speech, the voiced and unvoiced segments are separated and the energy content of the unvoiced frames and the onset-offset transitions is calculated in order to model the articulation process. This approach allows modeling the start and stop vibration of the vocal folds. The results show that, among the methods considered in this thesis, this approach is the most robust and accurate for the binary classification problem. The method is tested upon the three languages with recordings of isolated words, sentences, read texts, monologues, and the DDK evaluation. The accuracies ranged from 66 % to 99 %. The most consistent results of this approach among the three languages were obtained in the read texts with accuracies around 82 %, 80 %, and 94 % in Spanish, German, and Czech, respectively. (see Table 5.19), confirming the robustness and accuracy of the proposed method.

The DDK evaluations and the read texts of the three languages were used to perform several cross-language experiments, allowing to test the generalization capability of the proposed method. The experiments consisted on training the classifier with features extracted from recordings of one language and testing it on samples of another one. Additionally, some of the recordings of the test language were excluded from the test set and added to the training set incrementally (from 10 % to 80 %). According to the results, the accuracies range from 60 % to 99 % depending on the speech task, the added percentage of recordings, and the training language. The results obtained with the read texts are summarized in Figure 5.8 and the results with the rapid repetition of /pa-ta-ka/ are in Figure 5.10. In general, the accuracies are higher with recordings of /pa-ta-ka/. The best option to test the Spanish data is to add German recordings to the training set. Similarly, to test the German data, the best option is to add Spanish recordings to the training set. To test the Czech data, it seems that the best option is to add German recordings to the training set.

The prosodic characteristics of the speech of people with PD are modeled with a subset of sixty-four features of the Erlangen prosody module. These features are extracted from recordings of the isolated sentences, read texts, and monologues of the three languages. In order to use the prosody module independent to the spoken language, the speech unit defined for the computation of the features consisted on the voiced segments. The highest accuracy, 94 %, was obtained with the isolated sentences spoken in Czech. This sentences are actually questions, thus, it seems that the prosodic features are modeling the differences in the intonation of PD patients to pronounce questions. Unfortunately, the data considered for this thesis does not contain more recordings of questions to validate this finding in other languages.

The experiments addressed to estimate the neurological state of the Colombian patients are divided into two main parts. One consists on training and testing the regression model following a 10-fold cross validation strategy, and the other one consists on considering the same distribution of the data that was made for the organization of the ComParE 2015 challenge. In both experimental scenarios the three dimensions of speech are tested with recordings of read texts and monologues spoken in Spanish.

The parameters of the regression models build following the 10-fold cross validation procedure were optimized on test. It means that the results could be slightly optimistic; however, those results can be considered as the upper bound of the performance that can be obtained with the proposed methods in the PC-GITA database, and can help to state conclusions regarding the suitability of each speech dimension to estimate the neurological state of PD patients. The highest correlations are obtained with the prosody features extracted from the monologues ($\rho = 0.80$ and $r = 0.79$). Indicating that this dimension reflects the neurological state of the patients more accurately than the other two. The second dimension in the "ranking" was phonation extracted from read texts, with $\rho = 0.68$ and $r = 0.70$. Regarding the results obtained with the articulation features, the highest correlation values were obtained with the monologues ($\rho = 60$ and $r = 0.62$). The three dimensions were combined but the results were not higher than those obtained with the prosodic features. Finally, the features extracted from the monologues and the read texts were also merged and the correlations did not improved. All these results are summarized in Table 5.27.

The regression experiments that were performed with the data of the ComParE 2015 challenge include recordings of the fifty patients of the PC-GITA database and a set with eleven additional patients which were recorded in different acoustic conditions with respect to those of the PC-GITA data. For the optimization of the SVR parameters (C and ε), instead of doing 10-fold cross validation, in this case three subsets of data are defined i.e., train, development, and test. Thirty-five and fifteen recordings of the PC-GITA database are considered for train and development, respectively, and the recordings of the additional eleven patients are considered for test. The parameters of the regression models were optimized in the 'train vs development' experiments, avoiding biased and optimistic results. Additionally, the configuration of these experiments are closer to the real conditions, where the test samples are unknown and the acoustic conditions of the train set are not equal to those of the test set. The baseline of the challenge was computed considering a total of 6373 features of the 2.1. public release of the OpenSMILE toolkit. Forty-two speech tasks performed by each patient were considered including isolated words, sentences, read texts, and monologues, among others. The highest Spearman's correlation obtained in 'train vs development' was 0.49 with $\varepsilon = 1$ and $C = 10^{-3}$. For the 'train vs test' experiments the best result was 0.39 with $\varepsilon = 1$ and $C = 10^{-5}$. Note that the value of the parameter C had to be adjusted in the test process in order to obtained better results. If the C value would be kept equal to the value optimized in 'train vs development', the result would be a Spearman's correlation of 0.24.

The same data distribution of the ComParE 2015 was used to validate the suitability of the three speech dimensions analyzed in this thesis. These experiments only considered recordings of the read texts and monologues. The results indicate that phonation features extracted from the read texts are the most suitable to estimate the neurological state of the patients with a Spearman's correlation of 0.5 in 'train vs test'. This result is very interesting and promising not only because it overcomes the baseline of the challenge, but also because the feature set only includes measurements related with the phonation process, making easier the interpretation of the results. The second most suitable speech dimension comprises the proposed articulation features extracted from the monologues, with a Spearman's correlation of 0.39 in 'train vs test'. Among the group of measurements proposed to model articulation, the energy content of the onset transitions extracted from the monologues is the most suitable, with a Spearman's correlation of 0.39 in 'train vs test'. Regarding the results with the prosodic features, the correlation values obtained with this model were the lowest. This result can be explained by two possible reasons, one is that this modeling approach is being highly influenced by the change of the acoustic conditions of the test set, and the other reason could be that the speech unit defined to compute the prosodic features, which was the voiced segments, is not the most appropriate to do prosody modeling.

Chapter 6

Outlook

Phonation, articulation, and prosody characteristics have been evaluated in this thesis considering recordings with different speech tasks spoken in Spanish, German, and Czech. The Spanish data were collected during the development of this thesis and there are different lessons learned that are worth to be mentioned in order to help other researchers that are planning to record new data. Patient's medication records could point towards new research questions regarding the links between medication and speech. Although this could not be of the researchers interest, it is suggested to collect this information during the recordings sessions, however not evident it could be extremely hard to find afterwards. The recording protocol considered in this thesis was designed together with Neurologists, Phoniatricians, Phoneticians, and Engineers. It helped to have a protocol that considers aspects from different areas; however, those aspects related with the experience acquired after doing the experiments could not be considered. According to the results found, a recording protocol for assessing Parkinson's speech would include more tasks that force the patients to make particular articulatory movements that could evidence their difficulties to produce continuous speech e.g., phonemes like /p/, /t/, /k/, /b/, /m/, and /n/, among others. Similarly, more tasks regarding changes in the intonation like in questions and exclamations, could help to improve the results of prosodic features. One of the aims of this thesis was to assess PD speech in different languages considering characteristics of phonation, articulation, and prosody. To do the prosody analysis without any prior knowledge of the language spoken by the speakers, it was necessary to define the voiced segments as the speech unit to compute the prosodic features. According to the obtained results, it seems that the performance of the prosody analysis could increase if a different speech unit, for instance words or syllables, would be defined. This scenario was not considered in this thesis because its focus is on language-independent methods.

Further experiments to perform more detailed analyses regarding the articulatory capability of Parkinson's patients are required. For instance specific words or syllables could be grouped according to which articulator has to be moved to produce each sound. Doing such grouping would be possible to state strong conclusions regarding impairments in specific muscles and limbs that should be moved to produce those sounds. It could help to develop speech therapy exercises better adapted to the progress of each patient.

Multi-modal analysis could also help in the development of computer aided tools for the automatic and remote assessment of PD people. The integration of other signals in addition to the speech e.g., on-line writing, gait, and video, seem to be a promising alternative not only for monitoring Parkinson's patients but also elderly people in general.

Further to the potential trends mentioned above, the development of models adapted to the user i.e., user modeling, is another topic that could help for monitoring PD patients. To address this topic, it is necessary to continue recording and labeling patients. The labeling and recording processes can become expensive and time consuming; the involvement of a Neurologist expert increases the cost of the labeling process and keeping the special acoustic conditions could engage non negligible resources and time. In order to face this limitations, the algorithms and devices for the analysis and recording of speech signals have to be robust against different acoustic conditions. Ideally, the recording and analysis processes would be performed using a regular smart-phone or a cheap and portable device. A couple of recent publications ([Vasq 14] and [Vasq 15]) comprise some initial steps that have been done in this interesting and challenging topic.

Chapter 7

Summary

This work addresses the problems of automatic discrimination of people with Parkinson's disease (PD) and healthy controls and the prediction of the neurological state of the patients considering only speech recordings as prior knowledge of the speaker. The motivation for this work is to contribute in the development of computational methods for the assessment and monitoring of Parkinson's patients. This disease affects millions of people worldwide and the treatment cost increases every day. The development of computational tools that help the health systems to assess and monitor these population, could decrease the economic burden produced by this situation nowadays and could help the patients improving their quality of life. There are several works in the literature addressing different problems related with the speech of PD patients. Some of them are written mainly for medical experts and some others for engineers. This apparent difference in the two approaches makes difficult to propose methods from one "side" to impact the other one in order to contribute in the solution of the problem. The literature reviewed in this thesis highlights the gap between the clinical and engineering contributions, thus the methods and experiments proposed in this work try to contribute in closing such a gap with approaches motivated in clinical observations and validated with engineering and statistical methods. The characteristics of speech that are studied in this thesis are grouped into three dimensions: phonation, articulation, and prosody. Phonation reflects the capability of a speaker to produce air in the lungs to make the vocal folds vibrate and produce vocal sounds; articulation indicates the capability to move several muscles and limbs in order to produce specific sounds; and prosody analyzes mainly the intonation and timing performed by the speaker to produce natural speech.

Parkinson's disease is typically described as the result of the progressive loss of dopaminergic neurons in the substantia nigra of the mid brain. The loss of cholinergic neurons in the Striatum is also related with PD. Both types of cells are involved in the neurons activation in the motor cortex, and when this activation process does not work properly, the skills of the person to do motor activities are impaired i.e., movements with motor tremor or rigidity. Although there are also non-motor deficits observed in PD patients e.g., sleep, behavior, and emotion, among others, this thesis is only related with motor impairments. Such symptoms are evaluated by neurologists in the third part of the MDS-UPDRS scale. This scale is considered the global standard to assess PD patients and it is adopted in this thesis as the reference to validate the proposed methods. Although this part of the scale only considers the evaluation of speech in one of its thirty-three items, the main assumption made in this thesis is that there is a strong correlation between the scale and the speech impairments observed in PD patients.

Three different databases are considered for the validation of the methods studied in this thesis. Two of them contain recordings of German and Czech speakers, which were provided by Sabine Skodda [Skod 11b] and Jan Rusz [Rusz 13], respectively. The third database is called PC-GITA and it was built in Medellín, Colombia, during the development of this thesis. The database contains a total of one hundred Spanish native speakers, fifty PD patients and fifty healthy controls. The recordings were captured in a sound-proof booth and the speech tasks performed by the speakers are similar to those included in the German and Czech databases e.g., sustained vowels, rapid repetition of syllables, isolated words, sentences, monologues, and read texts, among others. PC-GITA database along with a set of recordings from eleven additional patients also recorded in Medellín, were used for the organization of the ComParE 2015 challenge, one of the special sessions of the INTERSPEECH.

The sets of measurements studied in this thesis are grouped into phonation, articulation, and prosody features. This grouping of features enables to state conclusions regarding specific phenomena in the speech of people with PD. The assessment of phonation includes features extracted from sustained vowels and from continuous speech signals. From sustained phonations, different measurements of periodicity, noise content, and nonlinear behavior are calculated. Additionally, several spectral-based measurements are computed also from sustained vowels to estimate the first two formants to evaluate the articulation capability of the patients. Periodicity and noise measurements are also used to analyze phonation from continuous speech signals, while the analysis of articulation in these recordings is performed by means of a method proposed in this thesis, which consists on the separation and characterization of voiced and unvoiced segments and the onset-offset transitions i.e. unvoiced to voiced and voiced to unvoiced. The main hypothesis behind this approach is that PD patients have difficulties to start and stop any kind of movement, thus those difficulties are also reflected when they try to start or stop the vibration of the vocal folds while speaking. The energy content of the unvoiced frames and the onset-offset transitions is modeled by means of twelve MFCCs and twenty-five energy bands which are scaled according to the Bark band scale i.e., Bark band energies (BBEs). Regarding the prosody analysis, a subset of sixty-four measurements extracted using the Erlangen prosody module is considered to model recordings of continuous speech signals spoken in the three languages. In order to do the prosodic analysis independent to the language, the voiced segments were defined as the speech units for the computation of the features. The method to discriminate between Parkinson's patients and healthy speakers is based on a soft-margin support vector machine (SM-SVM) with Gaussian kernel, with complexity parameter (C) and kernel band-width (σ). Regarding the experiments to predict the neurological state of the patients, a support vector regressor with a linear kernel and an ε-insensitive loss function (ε-SVR) is used.

The periodicity measurements extracted to model phonation from sustained vowels seem to be suitable for the discrimination between PD patients and healthy speakers. The obtained accuracies range from 81 % to 97 % depending on the vowel and the language. The accuracies obtained with the noise measurements and the nonlinear behavior features are around 75 %, indicating that these features need to be merged with other measurements like those based on periodicity in order to improve the results. Regarding the articulation analyses performed with sustained vowels, the first two formants (F_1 and F_2) along with several spectrum-based features are estimated. The accuracies are around 70 %, which indicates that the classical approaches for the assessment of articulation from sustained vowels are not suitable for the automatic discrimination of PD and HC. The recordings of continuous speech signals are also modeled with several phonation features like noise measurements and periodicity features e.g., jitter and shimmer, and the accuracies are around 70 % in most of the cases and around 85 % in some few experiments. These results show that phonation analysis in continuous speech signals could be suitable for the binary classification i.e. PD vs HC, however, the results are not consistent enough to state strong conclusions. Further experiments are performed with the energy measures extracted from the unvoiced segments and the onset-offset transitions of several continuous speech tasks including sentences, read texts, and monologues, among others. The results are around 95 % in most of the cases. These results are consistent through all the recordings of the three databases, which indicates that the method is robust against different noise conditions, and different languages. The result is interesting and very promising because it seems to reflect the difficulties observed in PD patients to start and stop the vibration of the vocal folds, which has a direct relation with clinical observations previously made by clinicians several years ago. Besides phonation and articulation, prosody analysis is also performed with recordings of the three languages. The results in read texts and monologues range from 68 % to 91 % depending on the language. The highest accuracy of the prosody features is 94 %, which is obtained with the Czech sentences. These utterances are actually questions, thus it seems that prosodic features are modeling differences in the intonation of PD patients to pronounce questions. Unfortunately, the datasets considered in this thesis do not include more questions to validate this finding in other languages.

The generalization capability of the method proposed to model the energy content of the unvoiced frames is tested in several cross-language experiments, with recordings of the rapid repetition of syllables and read texts of the three languages. The experiments consisted on training the classifier with samples of one language and test it on samples of another one. Additionally, some of the recordings of the test language are excluded from the test set and added to the training set incrementally (from 10 % to 80 %). According to the results, the accuracies range from 60 % to 99 % depending on the speech task, the added percentage of recordings, and the training language. In general, the accuracies are higher with recordings of /pa-ta-ka/. The best option to test the Spanish data is to train with German recordings. Similarly, when German recordings are used for training, the best results are obtained with the Spanish data. To test the Czech recordings, the best option is to train with the German data.

The three dimensions of speech considered for the automatic discrimination of PD patients and healthy speakers are also tested in the task of predicting the neurological state of the patients. The reference to estimate the neurological estate of the patients is the values of the MDS-UPDRS-III scale assigned by the Neurologist during the medical examination. The first prediction experiments consisted on consider only the fifty patients of the PC-GITA database and optimize the parameters of the regression model on the test set following a 10-fold cross validation strategy. Although the results obtained with this strategy are slightly optimistic, they can be considered as the upper bound of the performance that can be obtained with the methodology. A Spearman's correlation of $\rho = 0.8$ is obtained between the predicted and the actual state of the patients when the prosodic features extracted from the monologues are used. This is the highest correlation obtained in the regression experiments, and indicates that prosody is the dimension of speech that reflects more clearly the neurological state of the patients. The second highest correlation was $\rho = 0.68$, obtained with phonation features extracted from the read texts, which indicates that phonation can also reflect the neurological state of the patients. The results with articulation range between $\rho = 0.49$ and $\rho = 0.60$, depending on the speech task.

The second prediction experiment is based on the conditions of the ComParE 2015 challenge, which consists on training the models with the recordings of PC-GITA and test them with a set of eleven additional patients that were recorded also in Medellín but with different acoustic conditions i.e., yet not in a sound-proof booth but in a quiet office environments. These experiments enable testing the models in more realistic conditions, where the test patients are unknown and the acoustic conditions of the test set are different with respect to those of the train set. The correlation obtained with the phonation features extracted from read texts was $\rho = 0.5$, which is very interesting and promising because it overcomes the baseline of the challenge ($\rho = 0.39$) and because the feature set only includes measurements related with phonation, thus it is possible to state that the phonation process can reflect the neurological state of the PD patients better than the other two dimensions. Regarding the results obtained with the articulation features, the correlation was $\rho = 0.39$, which is also interesting because it pairs the challenge baseline and only includes those energy features that reflect the difficulty of the patients to start and stop the vibration of the vocal folds. Contrary to what was expected after the experiments with the 10-fold cross validation approach, the prosodic features did not show to be suitable to predict the neurological state of the test patients. This can be explained by two reasons, one is that the prosodic modeling is being highly influenced by the change of the acoustic conditions of the test set, and the other could be that the speech unit defined for the computation of the prosodic features is not appropriate to do prosody modeling.

Appendix A

Speech recording protocol

This appendix includes the original version of the protocol that was used to record the people in Medellín, Colombia, to build the PC-GITA database. As it was pointed out before, this recording protocol was designed together with experts from different areas, trying to include most of the ideas and hypotheses provided by each of them. However, after doing the preliminary experiments, it was realized that the speech tasks considered in this thesis comprise a representative sample of the exercises that we wanted to include since the beginning. Anyway, the speech tasks that were not considered during the development of this thesis can be used to address new research questions or to validate new hypotheses, thus it is a valuable data that can be exploited in the near future with academic proposes.

PROTOCOLO DE EVALUACIÓN FONOADIOLÓGICA PARA PACIENTES CON ENFERMEDAD DE PARKINSON

UNIVERSIDAD DE ANTIOQUIA – CLÍNICA NOEL

EVALUACIÓN DE LA FONACIÓN

1. Vocales sostenidas

Por favor pronuncie las vocales de forma sostenida (durante por lo menos 3 segundos o hasta que se le acabe el aire). Repita el ejercicio tres (3) veces					
Repetición 1	/a/	/e/	/i/	/o/	/u/
Repetición 2	/a/	/e/	/i/	/o/	/u/
Repetición 3	/a/	/e/	/i/	/o/	/u/

2. Vocales pronunciadas cambiando el tono

Por favor pronuncie las vocales cambiando el tono, tal y como se lo indica el fonoaudiólogo (una sola repetición)					
Alto – bajo - alto	/a/	/e/	/i/	/o/	/u/
Bajo – alto - bajo	/a/	/e/	/i/	/o/	/u/

Universidad de Antioquia
Medellín, Colombia

EVALUACIÓN DE LA ARTICULACIÓN
3. Análisis diadococinético (DDK)

Por favor repita rápidamente las siguientes palabras y sílabas.					
Pa-ta-ka	Pa-ka-ta	Pe-ta-ka	/pa/	/ta/	/ka/

4. Otras palabras

Por favor pronuncie las siguientes palabras					
petaka	Bodega	pato	apto	campana	Presa
plato	braso	blusa	trato	atleta	drama
grito	globo	crema	clavo	fruta	flecha
viaje	llueve	caucho	reina	ñame	coco
gato					

5. Verbos motores

Por favor pronuncie las siguientes palabras					
Acariciar	Aplaudir	Agarrar	Dibujar	Patalear	Pisotear
Trotar	Sonreír	Soplar	Masticar		

6. Sustantivos concretos

Por favor pronuncie las siguientes palabras					
Barco	Bosque	Ciudad	Establo	Hospital	Luna
Montaña	Nube	Puente	Tractor		

EVALUACIÓN DE PROSODIA

7. Repetición de frases (simple – compleja – simple - ...)

Por favor repita las siguientes frases	
1. Mi casa tiene tres cuartos	2. Omar, que vive cerca, trajo miel
3. Laura sube al tren que pasa	4. Los libros nuevos no caben en la mesa de la oficina
5. Rosita Niño, que pinta bien, donó sus cuadros ayer	6. Luisa Rey compra el colchón duro que tanto le gusta

8. Repetición de frases (compleja – simple – compleja - ...)

Por favor repita las siguientes frases	
1. Luisa Rey compra el colchón duro que tanto le gusta	2. Rosita Niño, que pinta bien, donó sus cuadros ayer
3. Los libros nuevos no caben en la mesa de la oficina	4. Laura sube al tren que pasa
5. Omar, que vive cerca, trajo miel	6. Mi casa tiene tres cuartos

9. Lectura de párrafo simple

Por favor lea el siguiente párrafo, haciendo las pausas y entonaciones donde indican los signos de puntuación, interrogación y admiración

Ayer fui al médico. ¿Qué le pasa? Me preguntó. Yo le dije: ¡Ay doctor! Donde pongo el dedo me duele. ¿Tiene la uña rota? Sí. Pues ya sabemos qué es. Deje su cheque a la salida.

FRASES CON ENTONACIÓN-EMOCIÓN

Por favor repita las siguientes frases

---

1. ¿Viste las noticias? Yo vi GANAR la medalla de plata en pesas. ¡Ese muchacho tiene mucha fuerza!

---

2. Juan se ROMPIÓ una PIERNA cuando iba en la MOTO.

---

3. Estoy muy triste, ayer vi MORIR a un amigo.

---

4. Estoy muy preocupado, cada vez me es más difícil HABLAR!

---

10. Monólogo: por lo menos 90 segundos

Por favor hable acerca de cómo es un día común y corriente en su vida, a qué hora se levanta, qué hace, qué come, etc.

Appendix B

Publications emerging from the development of this thesis

This appendix comprises a list of the most relevant publications derived from my doctoral studies. Of course all these papers are the result of the work and effort made by many people who helped me doing several things like some of the experiments, writing and/or correcting parts of the manuscripts, and discussing results, among others. I would like to thank specially Elkyn, Camilo, Tatiana, and Florian, because without their valuable contributions during the preparation of most of the manuscripts, it would not have been possible to publish them.

As in the beginning of my doctoral studies I did not have data from people with Parkinson's disease, there are some publications that correspond to experiments addressed with recordings of children with cleft lip and palate (CLP) or emotional speech signals. Although these experiments are not about PD, the methods reported in most of those publications were also tested later on Parkinson's patients, thus they are also part of the achievements of this thesis.

Publications related with Parkinson's disease

J.R. Orozco-Arroyave, F. Hönig, J.D. Arias-Londoño, J.F. Vargas-Bonilla, S. Skodda, J. Rusz, and E. Nöth, "Automatic detection of Parkinson's disease in running speech spoken in three different languages", under review in *Journal of the Acoustical Society of America (JASA)*, 2015.

J.R. Orozco-Arroyave, E.A. Belalcázar-Bolaños, J.D. Arias-Londoño, J.F. Vargas-Bonilla, S. Skodda, J. Rusz, F. Hönig, and E. Nöth, "Chracterization methods for the detection of multiple voice disorders: neurological, functional, and organic diseases", under review in *IEEE Journal of Biomedical and Health Informatics*, 2015.

J.R. Orozco-Arroyave, F. Hönig, J.D. Arias-Londoño, J.F. Vargas-Bonilla, and E. Nöth, "Spectral and cepstral analyzes for Parkinson's disease detection in Spanish vowels and words", *Expert Systems*, 2015. In press.

J.R. Orozco-Arroyave, F. Hönig, J.D. Arias-Londoño, J.F. Vargas-Bonilla, S. Skodda, J. Rusz, E. Nöth, "Voiced/unvoiced transitions in speech as a potential bio-marker to detect Parkinson's disease", In: *Proceedings of the 16th Annual Conference of the International Speech Communication Association (INTER-SPEECH)*, Dresden, Germany, 2015, In press.

J.C. Vásquez-Correa, T. Arias-Vergara, J.R. Orozco-Arroyave, J.F. Vargas-Bonilla, J.D. Arias-Londoño, and E. Nöth, "Automatic detection of Parkinson's disease from continuous speech recorded in non-controlled noise conditions", In: *Proceedings of the 16th Annual Conference of the International Speech Communication Association (INTERSPEECH)*, Dresden, Germany, 2015, In press.

B. Schuller and S. Steidl and A. Batliner and S. Hantke and F. Hönig and J. R. Orozco-Arroyave and E. Nöth and Y. Zhang and F. Weninger, "The INTER-SPEECH 2015 Computational Paralinguistics Challenge: Nativeness, Parkinson's & Eating Condition", In: *Proceedings of the 16th Annual Conference of the International Speech Communication Association (INTERSPEECH)*, Dresden, Germany, 2015, In press.

J.R. Orozco-Arroyave, N. García, J.F. Vargas-Bonilla, and E. Nöth, "Automatic detection of Parkinson's disease from compressed speech recordings", *Lecture Notes in Artificial Intelligence*, 2015, In press.

J.R. Orozco-Arroyave, T. Haderlein, and E. Nöth, "Automatic Detection of Parkinson's Disease in Reverberant Environments", *Lecture Notes in Artificial Intelligence*, 2015, In press.

J.C. Vásquez-Correa, J.R. Orozco-Arroyave, J.D. Arias-Londoño, J.F. Vargas-Bonilla, and E. Nöth, "New computer aided device for real time analysis of speech of people with Parkinson's disease", *Revista Facultad de Ingeniería UdeA*, No. 72, pp. 87-103, 2014.

J.R. Orozco-Arroyave, E.A. Belalcázar-Bolaños, J.D. Arias-Londoño, J.F. Vargas-Bonilla, T. Haderlein, and E. Nöth, "Phonation and articulation analysis of Spanish vowels for automatic detection of Parkinson's disease", *Lecture Notes in Artificial Intelligence*, Vol. 8655, pp. 389-296, 2014.

J.R. Orozco-Arroyave, J.D. Arias-Londoño, J.F. Vargas-Bonilla, M.C. González-Rátiva, E. Nöth, "New Spanish speech corpus database for the analysis of people suffering from Parkinson's disease", In: *Proceedings of the 9th Language Resources and Evaluation Conference (LREC)*, Reykjavik, Iceland, pp. 342-347, 2014.

J.R. Orozco-Arroyave, F. Hönig, J.D. Arias-Londoño, J.F. Vargas-Bonilla, S. Skodda, J. Rusz, and E. Nöth, "Automatic detection of Parkinson's disease from words uttered in three different languages", In: *Proceedings of the 15th Annual Conference of the International Speech Communication Association (INTERSPEECH)*, Singapore, pp. 1573-1577, 2014.

J.R. Orozco-Arroyave, "Multilingua system for the automatic detection of Parkinson's disease", *Doctoral Workshop on Speech Technology*, Google Inc., London, UK, 2014.

E.A. Belalcazar-Bolaños, J.R. Orozco-Arroyave, J.F. Vargas-Bonilla, J.D. Arias-Londoño, C.G. Castellanos-Domínguez and E. Nöth, "New cues in low-frequency of speech for Parkinson's disease detection", *Lecture Notes in Computer Science*, Vol. 7930, pp. 283-292, 2013.

J.R. Orozco-Arroyave, J.D. Arias-Londoño, J.F. Vargas-Bonilla and E. Nöth, "Perceptual analysis of speech signals from people with Parkinson's disease", *Lecture Notes in Computer Science*, Vol. 7930, pp. 201-211, 2013.

J.R. Orozco-Arroyave, J.D. Arias-Londoño, J.F. Vargas-Bonilla and E. Nöth, "Analysis of speech from people with Parkinson's disease through nonlinear dynamics", *Lecture Notes in Artificial Intelligence*, Vol. 7911, pp. 112-119, 2013.

Publications related with CLP and emotional speech

J.R. Orozco-Arroyave, J.F. Vargas-Bonilla, J.C. Vásquez-Correa, G. Castellanos-Domínguez, E. Nöth, "Automatic assessment of hypernasal speech of children with cleft lip and palate from Spanish vowels and words using classical measures and nonlinear analysis", under review in *Revista Facultad de Ingeniería UdeA*, 2015.

P. Henríquez, J.B. Alonso-Hernández, M.A. Ferrer-Ballester, C.M. Travieso-González and J.R. Orozco-Arroyave, "Nonlinear Dynamics Characterization of Emotional Speech", *Neurocomputing*, Vol. 132, pp. 126-135, 2014.

J.R. Orozco-Arroyave, J.F. Vargas-Bonilla, J.D. Arias-Londoño, S. Murillo-Rendón, G. Castellanos-Domínguez, and J.F. Garcés, "Nonlinear dynamics for hypernasality detection in Spanish vowels and words", *Cognitive Computation*, Vol. 5, No. 4, pp. 448-457, 2013.

P. Henríquez-Rodríguez, J.B. Alonso-Hernández, M.A. Ferrer-Ballester, C.M. Travieso-González, and J.R. Orozco-Arroyave, "Global selection of features for nonlinear dynamics characterization of emotional speech", *Cognitive Computation*, Vol. 5, No. 4, pp. 517-525, 2013.

C.M. Travieso-González, J.B. Alonso-Hernández, J.R. Orozco-Arroyave, J. Solé-Casals, and E. Gallego-Jutglá, "Automatic detection of laryngeal pathologies in running speech based on the HMM transformation of the nonlinear dynamics", *Lecture Notes in Artificial Intelligence*, Vol. 7911, pp. 136-143, 2013.

J.R. Orozco-Arroyave, J.D. Arias-Londoño, J.F. Vargas-Bonilla, and E. Nöth, "Automatic detection of hypernasal speech signals using nonlinear and entropy measurements", In: *Proceedings of the 13th Annual Conference of the International Speech Communication Association (INTERSPEECH)*, Portland, USA, pp. 2029-2032, 2012.

List of Figures

List of Tables

Bibliography

[Acke 89]   H. Ackermann, W. Ziegler, and W. H. Oertel. "Palilalia as a symptom of le-
            vodopa induced hyperkinesia in Parkinson's disease". *Journal of Neurology,
            Neurosurgery, and Psychiatry*, Vol. 52, No. 6, pp. 805–807, 1989.

[Acke 91]   H. Ackermann and W. Ziegler. "Articulatory deficits in Parkinsonian dysarth-
            ria: an acoustic analysis". *Journal of Neurology, Neurosurgery, and Psychiatry*,
            Vol. 54, No. 12, pp. 1093–1088, 1991.

[Aize 64]   A. Aizerman, E. M. Braverman, and L. I. Rozoner. "Theoretical foundations
            of the potential function method in pattern recognition learning". *Automation
            and Remote Control*, No. 25, p. 821–837, 1964.

[Alon 05]   J. B. Alonso, J. de León, I. Alonso, and M. A. Ferrer. "Using nonlinear features
            for voice disorder detection". In: *NOLISP*, pp. 94–106, 2005.

[Alve 05]   G. Alves, T. Wentzel-Larsen, D. Aarsland, and J. P. Larsen. "Progression
            of motor impairment and disability in Parkinson disease: A population-based
            study". *Neurology*, Vol. 65, No. 9, pp. 1436–1441, 2005.

[Aria 10]   J. D. Arias-Londoño, J. I. Godino-Llorente, N. Sáenz-Lechón, V. Osma-Ruiz,
            and C. G. Castellanos-Domínguez. "An improved method for voice pathology
            detection by means of a HMM-based feature space transformation". *Pattern
            Recognition*, Vol. 42, No. 2010, pp. 3100–3112, 2010.

[Aria 11]   J. D. Arias-Londoño, J. I. Godino-Llorente, N. Sáenz-Lechón, V. Osma-Ruiz,
            and G. Castellanos-Domínguez. "Automatic detection of pathological voices
            using complexity measures, noise parameters, and mel-cepstral coefficients.".
            IEEE Transactions on Biomedical Engineering, Vol. 58, No. 2, pp. 370–9,
            2011.

[Bang 03]   V. Bangert, V. Hermsen, N. Stigler, R. Stille, and S. Wigman. *De Pitch Limiting
            Voice Treatment: Stemtherapie voor patiënten met de ziekte van Parkinson.*
            HAN University of Applied Sciences, Nijmegen, 2003.

[Batl 00]   A. Batliner, R. Huber, H. Niemann, E. Nöth, J. Spilker, and K. Fischer. "Verb-
            mobil: foundations of speech-to-text translation". In: W. Wahlser, Ed., *The Re-
            cognition of Emotion*, pp. 122–130, Springer-Verlag, Berlin, Germany, 2000.

[Batl 03]   A. Batliner, K. Fischer, R. Huber, J. Spilker, and E. Nöth. "How to find trouble
            in communication". *Speech Communication*, Vol. 40, No. 1–2, pp. 117–143,
            2003.

[Baye 15]   A. Bayestehtashk, M. Asgari, I. Shafran, and J. Mcnames. "Fully automated
            assessment of the severity of Parkinson's disease from speech". *Computer
            Speech & Language*, Vol. 29, No. 1, pp. 172–185, 2015.

[Bela 13]   E. A. Belalcázar-Bolaños, J. R. Orozco-Arroyave, J. F. Vargas-Bonilla, J. D. Arias-Londoño, C. Castellanos-Domínguez, and E. Nöth. "New cues in low-frequency of speech for automatic detection of Parkinson's disease". *Lecture Notes in Computer Science*, No. 7930, pp. 283–292, 2013.

[Benk 00]   T. Benke, C. Hohenstein, W. Poewe, and B. Butterworth. "Repetitive speech phenomena in Parkinson's disease". *Journal of Neurology Neurosurgery and Psychiatry*, Vol. 69, pp. 319–325, 2000.

[Bock 13]   T. Bocklet, S. Steidl, E. Nöth, and S. Skodda. "Automatic evaluation of Parkinson's speech - acoustic, prosodic and voice related cues". In: *Proceedings of the 14th Annual Conference of the International Speech Communication Association (INTERSPEECH)*, pp. 1149–1153, Lyon, France, 2013.

[Boer 01]   P. Boersma and D. Weenink. "PRAAT, a system for doing phonetics by computer". *Glot International*, Vol. 5, No. 9/10, pp. 341–345, 2001.

[Boer 93]   P. Boersma. "Accurate short-term analysis of the fundamental frequency and the harmonics-to noise-ratio of a sampled sound". *Institute of Phonetic Sciences, University of Amsterdam*, Vol. 17, pp. 97–110, 1993.

[Bose 92]   B. E. Boser, I. M. Guyon, and V. Vapnik. "A training algorithm for optimal margin classifiers". In: *Proceedings of 5th Annual Workshop on Computational Learning Theory*, p. 144–152, ACM, Pittsburgh, USA, 1992.

[Boya 97]   B. Boyanov and S. Hadjitodorov. "Acoustic analysis of pathological voices. A voice analysis system for the screening of laryngeal disease". *IEEE Engineering in Medicine and Biology Magazine*, Vol. 16, No. 4, pp. 74–82, 1997.

[Cair 96]   D. A. Cairns, J. H. Hansen, and J. E. Riski. "A noninvasive technique for detecting hypernasal speech using a nonlinear operator". *IEEE Transactions on Biomedical Engineering*, Vol. 43, No. 1, pp. 35–45, 1996.

[Cant 63]   G. J. Canter. "Speech characteristics of patients with Parkinson's disease: I. Intensity, pitch, and duration". *Journal of Speech and Hearing Disorders*, Vol. 28, No. 3, pp. 221–229, 1963.

[Cant 65a] G. J. Canter. "Speech characteristics of patients with Parkinson's disease: II. Physiological support for speech". *Journal of Speech and Hearing Disorders*, Vol. 30, No. 1, pp. 44–49, 1965.

[Cant 65b] G. J. Canter. "Speech characteristics of patients with Parkinson's disease: III. articulation, diadochokinesis, and over-all speech adequacy". *Journal of Speech and Hearing Disorders*, Vol. 30, No. 3, pp. 217–224, 1965.

[Caru 13]   A. Carullo, A. Vallan, and A. Astolfi. "Design issues for a portable vocal analyzer". *IEEE Transactions on Instrumentation and Measurement*, Vol. 62, No. 5, pp. 1084–1093, 2013.

[Chen 11]   K. Chenausky, J. Macauslan, and R. Goldhor. "Acoustic analysis of PD speech". *Parkinson's Disease*, Vol. 2011, p. 435232, 2011.

[Cort 95]   C. Cortes and V. Vapnik. "Support vector networks". *Machine Learning*, No. 20, pp. 273–297, 1995.

[Cost 05]   M. Costa, A. Goldberger, and C. Peng. "Multiscale entropy analysis of biological signals". *Physical Review E*, Vol. 71, pp. 1–18, 2005.

[Crit 81]   E. M. Critchley. "Speech disorders of Parkinsonism: a review". *Journal of Neurology, Neurosurgery, and Psychiatry*, Vol. 44, No. 9, pp. 751–758, 1981.

[Darl 69]   F. Darley, A. Aronson, and J. Brown. "Clusters of deviant speech dimensions in the dysarthrias". *Journal of Speech Language and Hearing Research*, Vol. 12, pp. 462–496, 1969.

[Davi 80]   S. Davis and P. Mermelstein. "Comparison of parametric representations for monosyllabic word recognition in continuously spoken sentences". *IEEE Transactions on Acoustics, Speech, and Signal Processing*, Vol. 28, No. 4, 1980.

[de S 03]   B. J. M. de Swart, S. C. Willemse, B. A. M. Maassen, and M. W. I. M. Horstink. "Improvement of voicing in patients with Parkinson's disease by speech therapy". *Neurology*, Vol. 60, No. 3, pp. 498–500, 2003.

[Di N 06]   V. Di Nicola, M. L. Fiorella, D. A. Spinelli, and R. Fiorella. "Acoustic analysis of voice in patients treated by reconstructive subtotal laryngectomy. Evaluation and critical review". *Acta Otorhinolaryngologica Italica*, Vol. 26, No. 2, pp. 59–68, 2006.

[Duff 00]   J. R. Duffy. "Motor speech disorders: clues to neurologic diagnosis". In: *Parkinson's Disease and Movement Disorders: Diagnosis and Treatment Guidelines for the Practicing Physician*, pp. 35–53, Mayo Foundation for Medical Education and Research, 2000.

[Duff 95]   J. R. Duffy. *Speech motor disorders: substrates, differential diagnosis, and management*. Elsevier, Morby, St. Louis, 1st Ed., 1995.

[Eybe 10]   F. Eyben, M. Wöllmer, and B. Shuller. "openSMILE - The Munich versatile and fast open-source audio feature extractor". In: *Proceedings of the ACM Multimedia*, pp. 1459–1462, New York, USA, 2010.

[Eybe 13]   F. Eyben, F. Weninger, F. Groß, and B. Schuller. "Recent developments in openSMILE, the Munich open-source multimedia feature extractor". In: *Proceedings of ACM MM*, pp. 835–838, ACM, Barcelona, Spain, October 2013.

[Fair 60]   G. Fairbanks. *Voice and Articulation Drill Book*. Harper and Brothers, 1960. 2nd ed. New York.

[Flas 12]   A. Flasskamp, S. Kotz, U. Schlegel, and S. Skodda. "Acceleration of syllable repetition in Parkinson's disease is more prominent in the left-side dominant patients". *Parkinsonism & Related Disorders*, Vol. 18, No. 4, pp. 343–7, 2012.

[Forr 89]   K. Forrest, G. Weismer, and G. Turner. "Kinematic, Acoustic and Perceptual Analyses of Connected Speech Produced by Parkinsonian and Normal Geriatric Males". *Journal of the Acoustic Society of America*, No. 85, pp. 2608–2622, 1989.

[Fras 86]   A. M. Fraser and H. L. Swinney. "Independent coordinates for strange attractors from mutual information". *Physical Review A*, Vol. 33, No. 2, pp. 1134–1140, 1986.

[Gall 02]   F. Gallwitz, H. Niemann, E. Nöth, and V. Warnke. "Integrated recognition of words and prosodic phrase boundaries". *Speech Communication*, Vol. 36, No. 1–2, pp. 81–95, 2002.

[Gamb 97] J. Gamboa, F. J. Jiménez-Jiménez, A. Nieto, J. Montojo, M. Ortí-Pareja, J. A. Molina, E. García-Albea, and I. Cobeta. "Acoustic voice analysis in patients with Parkinson's disease treated with dopaminergic drugs". *Journal of Voice*, Vol. 11, No. 3, pp. 314–320, 1997.

[Gobe 05] A. M. Goberman and E. Lawrence. "Acoustic Analysis of Clear Versus Conversational Speech in Individuals with Parkinson Disease". *Journal of Communication Disorders*, Vol. 38, No. 3, pp. 215–230, 2005.

[Gobe 08] A. M. Goberman and M. Blomgren. "Fundamental frequency change during offset and onset of voicing in individuals with Parkinson disease". *Journal of Voice*, Vol. 22, No. 2, pp. 178–191, 2008.

[Godi 06] J. I. Godino-Llorente, P. Gómez-Vilda, and M. Blanco-Velasco. "Dimensionality reduction of a pathological voice quality assessment system based on Gaussian mixture models and short-term cepstral parameters". *IEEE transactions on biomedical engineering*, Vol. 53, No. 10, pp. 1943–1953, 2006.

[Goet 04] C. G. Goetz, W. Poewe, O. Rascol, C. Sampaio, G. T. Stebbins, C. Counsell, N. Giladi, R. G. Holloway, C. G. Moore, G. K. Wenning, M. Yahr, and L. Seidl. "Movement Disorder Society task force report on the Hoehn and Yahr staging scale: status and recommendations". *Movement Disorders*, Vol. 19, No. 9, pp. 1020–1028, 2004.

[Goet 08] C. G. Goetz and et al. "Movement Disorder Society-sponsored revision of the Unified Parkinson's Disease Rating Scale (MDS-UPDRS): scale presentation and clinimetric testing results". *Movement Disorders*, Vol. 23, No. 15, pp. 2129–2170, 2008.

[Goet 09] C. G. Goetz and et al. "Testing objective measures of motor impairment in early Parkinson's disease: feasibility study of an at-home testing device". *Movement Disorders*, Vol. 24, No. 4, pp. 551–556, 2009.

[Gold 01] K. K. Golding. *Therapy techniques for cleft palate speech and related disorders*. Singular Thomson Learning, San Diego, 2001.

[Grop 12] M. Gropp. *Smart combination of individual predictions for the assessment of non-native prosody*. Pattern Recognition Lab, Friedrich-Alexander-Universität Erlangen-Nürnberg, Erlangen, Germany, 2012.

[Hade 07] T. Haderlein. *Automatic evaluation of tracheoesophageal substitute voices, volume 25 of Studien zur Mustererkennung*. Logos Verlag, Berlin, Germany, 2007.

[Hade 15] T. Haderlein, M. Döllinger, V. Matoušek, and E. Nöth. "Objective voice and speech analysis of persons with chronic hoarseness by prosodic analysis of speech samples". *Logopedics Phoniatrics Vocology*, No. February, pp. 1–11, 2015.

[Hall 57] M. Halle, G. Hughes, and J. Radley. "Acoustic properties of stop consonants". *Journal of the Acoustical Society of America*, Vol. 29, No. 1, pp. 107–116, 1957.

[Hast 01] T. Hastie, R. Tibshirani, and J. H. Friedman. *The elements of statistical learning: data mining, inference, and prediction*. Springer-Verlag, New York, 2001.

[Herm 90] H. Hermansky. "Perceptual linear predictive (PLP) analysis of speech". *Journal of the Acoustical Society of America*, Vol. 87, No. 4, pp. 1738–1752, 1990.

[Herm 94]   H. Hermansky and N. Morgan. "RASTA processing of speech". *IEEE transactions on speech and audio processing*, Vol. 2, No. 4, pp. 578–589, 1994.

[Herz 94]   H. Herzel, D. Berry, and I. R. Titze. "Analysis of vocal disorders with methods from nonlinear dynamics". *Journal of Speech and Hearing Research*, Vol. 37, No. 2, pp. 1008–1019, 1994.

[Honi 05]   F. Hönig, G. Stemmer, C. Hacker, and F. Brugnara. "Revising Perceptual Linear Prediction (PLP)". In: *Proceedings of the 6th European Conference on Speech Communication and Technology (EUROSPEECH)*, pp. 2997–3000, Lisbon, Portugal, 2005.

[Horn 98]   O. Hornykiewicz. "Biochemical aspects of Parkinson's disease". *Neurology*, Vol. 51, No. 2, pp. S2–S9, 1998.

[Hube 00]   C. J. Huberty and L. L. Lowman. "Group overlap as a basis for effect size". *Educational and Psychological Measurement*, Vol. 60, No. 4, pp. 543–563, 2000.

[Hube 02]   R. Huber. *Prosodisch-linguistische klassifikation von emotion, volume 8 of studien zur Mustererkennung*. Logos Verlag, Berlin, Germany, 2002.

[Jack 99]   J. Jack, O. Timothy, H. J. Chen, J. I. Stem, D. Vlagos, and D. Hanson. "Aerodynamic measurements of pPatients with Parkinson's disease". *Journal of Voice*, Vol. 13, No. 4, pp. 583–591, 1999.

[Jian 06]   J. Jiang, Y. Zhang, and C. McGilligan. "Chaos in voice, from modeling to measurement". *Journal of Voice*, Vol. 20, No. 1, pp. 2–17, 2006.

[Jime 97]   F. J. Jiménez-Jiménez, J. Gamboa, A. Nieto, J. Guerrero, M. Ortí-Pareja, J. Molinas, E. García-Albea, and I. Cobeta. "Acoustic voice analysis in untreated with Parkinson's disease". *Parkinsonism & Related Disorders*, Vol. 3, No. 2, pp. 111–116, 1997.

[John 13a] S. J. Johnson., M. Diener, A. Kaltenboeck, H. G. Birnbaum, and A. D. Siderowf. "An economic model of Parkinson's disease: Implications for slowing progression in the United States". *Movement Disorders*, Vol. 28, No. 3, pp. 319–326, 2013.

[John 13b] S. J. Johnson, A. Kaltenboeck, M. Diener, H. G. Birnbaum, E. Grubb, J. Castelli-Haley, and A. D. Siderowf. "Costs of parkinson's disease in a privately insured population". *PharmacoEconomics*, Vol. 31, No. 9, pp. 799–806, 2013.

[Kant 06]   H. Kantz and T. Schreiber. *Nonlinear time series analysis*. Cambridge, U.K: Cambridge University Press, 2nd Ed., 2006.

[Karu 39]   W. Karush. *Minima of functions of several variables with inequalities as side constraints*. Dept. of Mathematics, University of Chicago, Chicago, Illinois, 1939.

[Kasp 87]   F. Kaspar and H. Shuster. "Easily calculable measure for complexity of spatiotemporal patterns". *Physical Review A*, Vol. 36, No. 2, pp. 842–848, 1987.

[Kasu 86]   H. Kasuya, S. Ogawa, K. Mashima, and S. Ebihara. "Normalized noise energy as an acoustic measure to evaluate pathologic voice". *Journal of the Acoustical Society of America*, Vol. 80, No. 5, pp. 1329–1334, 1986.

[Kenn 92]   M. B. Kennel, R. Brown, and H. D. I. Abarbanel. "Determining embedding dimension for phase-space reconstruction using geometrical construction". *Physical Review A*, Vol. 45, No. 6, pp. 3403–3411, 1992.

[Kent 99]   R. Kent, G. Weismer, J. Kent, H. Vorperian, and J. Duffy. "Acoustic studies of dysarthric speech: methods, progress, and potential.". *Journal of Communication Disorders*, Vol. 32, No. 3, pp. 141–186, 1999.

[Kim 00]   H. Kim, S. Choi, and H. Lee. "On approximating line spectral frequencies to LPC cepstral coefficients". *IEEE transactions on speech and audio processing*, Vol. 8, No. 2, pp. 195–199, 2000.

[King 94]   J. King, L. Ramig, J. Lemke, and Y. Horii. "Parkinson disease: longitudinal changes in acoustic parameters of phonation". *Journal of Medical Speech-Language Pathology*, Vol. 2, pp. 29–42, 1994.

[Kuhn 51]   H. W. Kuhn and A. W. Tucker. "Nonlinear programming". In: *Proceedings of 2nd Berkeley Symposium*, pp. 481–492, University of California Press, Berkeley, USA, 1951.

[Le D 98]   G. Le Dorze, J. Ryalls, C. Brassard, N. Boulanger, and D. Ratté. "A comparison of the prosodic characteristics of the speech of people with Parkinson's disease and Friedrich's ataxia with neurologically normal speakers". *Folia Phoniatrica et Logopaedica*, Vol. , No. 50, pp. 1–9, 1998.

[Lemp 76]   A. Lempel and J. Ziv. "On the complexity of finite sequences". *IEEE Transactions on Information Theory*, No. 22, pp. 75–81, 1976.

[Litt 07]   M. Little, P. McSharry, S. Roberts, D. Costello, and I. Moroz. "Exploiting nonlinear recurrence and fractal scaling properties for voice disorder detection". *Biomedical Engineering Online*, Vol. 6, No. , p. 23, 2007.

[Litt 09]   M. Little, P. McSharry, E. Hunter, J. Spielman, and L. Ramig. "Suitability of dysphonia measurements for telemonitoring of Parkinson's disease". *IEEE Transactions on Biomedical Engineering*, Vol. 56, No. 4, pp. 1015–1022, 2009.

[Loge 78]   J. Logemann, H. Fisher, B. Boshes, and E. Blonsky. "Frequency and cooccurrence of vocal tract dysfunctions in the speech of a large sample of Parkinson patients". *Journal of Speech and Hearing Disorders*, Vol. 43, No. , pp. 47–57, 1978.

[Loge 81]   J. A. Logemann and H. B. Fisher. "Vocal tract control in Parkinson's disease: phonetic feature analysis of misarticulations". *Journal of Speech and Hearing Disorders*, Vol. 46, No. 4, pp. 348–452, 1981.

[Maie 09]   A. Maier, F. Hönig, V. Zeissler, A. Batliner, E. Körner, N. Yamanaka, P. Ackermann, and E. Nöth. "A language-independent feature set for the automatic evaluation of prosody". In: *Proceedings of the 10th Annual Conference of the International Speech Communication Association (INTERSPEECH)*, pp. 600–603, Brighton, UK, 2009.

[Mart 11]   P. Martínez-Martín, C. Rodríguez-Blázquez, M. M. Kurtis, and K. R. Chaudhuri. "The impact of non-motor symptoms on health-related quality of life of patients with Parkinson's disease". *Movement Disorders*, Vol. 26, pp. 299–406, 2011.

[Mart 14]   P. Martínez-Martín, C. Rodríguez-Blázquez, M. J. Forjaz, and K. R. Chaudhuri. "Multi-domain scales". In: *Guide to assessment scales in Parkinson's disease*, pp. 13–23, Springer Healthcare Ltd, London, UK, 2014.

[Mera 05]   A. L. Merati, Y. D. Heman-Ackah, M. Abaza, K. W. Altman, L. Sulica, and S. Belamowicz. "Common movement disorders affecting the larynx: a report from the neurolaryngology committee of the AAO-HNS". *Otolaryngology– Head and Neck Surgery*, Vol. 133, No. 5, pp. 654–65, Nov. 2005.

[Mich 97]   D. Michaelis, T. Gramss, and H. Strube. "Glottal-to-noise excitation ratio- a new measure for describing pathological voices". *Acustica/ActaAcustica*, Vol. 83, No. , pp. 700–706, 1997.

[Mobe 08]   J. Möbes, G. Joppich, F. Stiebritz, R. Dengler, and C. Schröder. "Emotional speech in Parkinson's disease". *Movement Disorders*, Vol. 23, No. 6, pp. 824– 829, 2008.

[Move 03]   Movement Disorder Society. "State of the art review the Unified Parkinson's Disease Rating Scale (UPDRS): status and recommendations". *Movement Disorders*, Vol. 18, No. 7, pp. 738–750, 2003.

[Muri 11]   S. Murillo-Rendón, J. R. Orozco-Arroyave, J. D. Arias-Londoño, J. F. Vargas-Bonilla, and G. Castellanos-Domínguez. "Automatic detection of hypernasality in children". *Lecture Notes in Artificial Intelligence*, Vol. 6687, pp. 167– 174, 2011.

[Murp 05]   P. J. Murphy and O. O. Akande. "Quantification of glottal and voiced speech harmonics-to-noise ratios using cepstral-based estimation". In: *Procedings of the NOLISP*, pp. 1–9, 2005.

[Murt 91]   H. A. Murthy and B. Yegnanaryana. "Formant extraction from group delay function". *Speech Communication*, Vol. 10, No. 1991, pp. 209–221, 1991.

[Nati 06]   National Collaborating Centre for Chronic Conditions. *Parkinson's disease*. Royal College of Physicians, London, UK., 2006.

[Noth 00]   E. Nöth, A. Batliner, A. Kießling, R. Kompe, and H. Niemann. "VERB-MOBIL: The use of prosody in the linguistic components of a speech understanding System". *IEEE Transactions on Speech and Audio Processing*, Vol. 8, No. 5, pp. 519–532, 2000.

[Noth 02]   E. Nöth, A. Batliner, V. Warnke, J. Haas, M. Boros, J. Buckow, R. Huber, F. Gallwitz, M. Nutt, and H. Niemann. "On the use of prosody in automatic dialogue understanding". *Speech Communication*, Vol. 36, No. 1–2, pp. 45–62, 2002.

[Noth 11]   E. Nöth, A. Maier, A. Gebhard, and T. Bocklet. "Automatic evaluation of dysarthric speech and telemedical use in therapy". *The Phonetician*, Vol. 103, No. 1, pp. 75–87, 2011.

[Noth 99]   E. Nöth, A. Batliner, A. Kießling, R. Kompe, and H. Niemann. "Suprasegmental modelling". In: K. Ponting, Ed., *Computational Models of Speech Pattern Processing*, pp. 182–199, Springer-Verlag, Berlin, Germany, 1999.

[Novo 14]   M. Novotný, J. Rusz, R. Čmejla, and E. Růžička. "Automatic evaluation of articulatory aisorders in Parkinson's disease". *IEEE/ACM Transactions on Audio, Speech, and Language Processing*, Vol. 22, No. 9, pp. 1366–1378, 2014.

[Oroz 11]   J. R. Orozco-Arroyave. *Análisis acústico y de dinámica no lineal para la detección de hipernasalidad en la voz*. Master Thesis, Faculty of Engineering, Universidad de Antioquia, Medellín, Colombia, December 2011.

[Oroz 13a]   J. R. Orozco-Arroyave, J. D. Arias-Londoño, J. F. Vargas-Bonilla, and E. Nöth. "Analysis of speech from people with Parkinson's disease through nonlinear dynamics". *Lecture Notes in Artificial Intelligence*, Vol. 7911, pp. 112–119, 2013.

[Oroz 13b]   J. R. Orozco-Arroyave, J. F. Vargas-Bonilla, J. D. Arias-Londoño, S. Murillo-Rendón, G. Castellanos-Domínguez, and J. F. Garcés. "Nonlinear dynamics for hypernasality detection in spanish vowels and words". *Cognitive Computation*, Vol. 5, No. 4, pp. 448–457, 2013.

[Oroz 14a]   J. R. Orozco-Arroyave. "Multilingual system for the automatic detection of Parkinson's disease". April 2014. Doctoral workshop on Speech Technology, Google Inc.

[Oroz 14b]   J. R. Orozco-Arroyave, E. A. Belalcázar-Bolaños, J. D. Arias-Londoño, J. F. Vargas-Bonilla, T. Haderlein, and E. Nöth. "Phonation and articulation analysis of Spanish vowels for automatic detection of Parkinson's disease". *Lecture Notes in Artificial Intelligence*, No. 8655, pp. 374–381, 2014.

[Oroz 14c]   J. R. Orozco-Arroyave, F. Hönig, J. D. Arias-Londoño, J. F. Vargas-Bonilla, S. Skodda, J. Rusz, and E. Nöth. "Automatic detection of Parkinson's disease from words uttered in three different languages". In: *Proceedings of the 15th Annual Conference of the International Speech Communication Association (INTERSPEECH)*, pp. 1473–1577, Singapore, 2014.

[Oroz 15a]   J. R. Orozco-Arroyave, F. Hönig, J. D. Arias-Londoño, J. F. Vargas-Bonilla, and E. Nöth. "Spectral and cepstral analyses for Parkinson's disease detection in Spanish vowels and words". *Expert Systems*, pp. 1–10, 2015.

[Oroz 15b]   J. R. Orozco-Arroyave, F. Hönig, J. D. Arias-Londoño, J. F. Vargas-Bonilla, S. Skodda, J. Rusz, and E. Nöth. "Voiced/unvoiced transitions in speech as a potential bio-marker to detect Parkinson's disease". In: *Proceedings of the 16th Annual Conference of the International Speech Communication Association (INTERSPEECH)*, Dresden, Germany, 2015.

[Osel 68]   V. A. Oseledec. "A multiplicative ergodic theorem. Lyapunov characteristic numbers for dynamical systems". *Transactions of Moscow Mathematic Society*, Vol. 19, pp. 197–231, 1968.

[Park 17]   J. Parkinson. *An essay on the Shaking Palsy*. Whittingham and Rowland, 1817.

[Pate 09]   R. Patel and P. Campellone. "Acoustic and perceptual cues to contrastive stress in dysarthria". *Journal of Speech, Language, and Hearing Research*, Vol. 52, pp. 206–222, 2009.

[Pere 96]   K. S. Perez, L. O. Ramig, M. E. Smith, and C. Dromery. "The Parkinson larynx: tremor and videostroboscopic findings". *Journal of Voice*, Vol. 10, No. 4, pp. 353–361, 1996.

[Rami 01]   L. O. Ramig, S. Sapir, S. Countryman, A. A. Pawlas, C. O. Brien, M. Hoehn, L. L. Thompson, and W. J. Gould. "Intensive voice treatment (LSVT) for patients with Parkinson's pisease: a 2 year follow up". *Journal of Neurology, Neurosurgery, and Psychiatry*, Vol. 71, pp. 493–498, 2001.

[Rami 08]   L. O. Ramig, C. Fox, and S. Sapir. "Speech Treatment for Parkinson's Disease". *Expert Review Neurotherapeutics*, Vol. 8, No. 2, pp. 297–309, 2008.

[Rami 88] L. O. Ramig, C. Mead, Y. H. R. Scherer, K. Larson, and D. Kohler. "Voice therapy and Parkinson's disease: a longitudinal study of efficacy". In: *Proceedings
of the Clinical Dysarthria Conference*, San Diego, USA, 1988.

[Rami 94] L. Ramig, C. Bonitati, J. Lemke, and Y. Horii. "Voice therapy for patients
with Parkinson's disease: development of an approach and preliminary efficacy
data". *Journal of Medical Speech-Language Pathology*, Vol. 2, pp. 191–210,
1994.

[Resc 07] B. Resch, M. Nilsson, A. Ekmann, and W. Kleijn. "Estimation of the instant-
aneous pitch of speech". *IEEE Transactions on Audio, Speech, and Language
Processing*, Vol. 15, No. 3, pp. 813–822, 2007.

[Rich 00] J. S. Richman and J. R. Moorman. "Physiological time-series analysis using
approximate entropy and sample entropy". *Am J Physiol Heart Circ Physiol*,
Vol. 279, pp. H2039–H2049, 2000.

[Rijk 00] M. de Rijk. "Prevalence of Parkinson's disease in Europe: A collaborative
study of population-based cohorts". *Neurology*, Vol. 54, pp. 21–23, 2000.

[Robb 86] J. A. Robbins, J. A. Logemann, and H. S. Kirshner. "Swallowing and speech
production in Parkinson's disease". *Annals of Neurology*, Vol. 19, No. 3,
pp. 283–287, 1986.

[Rubo 85] R. Rubow and E. Swift. "A microcomputer-based wearable bio-feedback
device to improve transfer of treatment in Parkinsonian dysarthria". *Journal of
Speech and Hearing Disorders*, Vol. 50, No. 2, pp. 178–185, 1985.

[Rusz 11] J. Rusz, R. Cmejla, H. Ruzickova, and E. Ruzicka. "Quantitative acoustic
measurements for characterization of speech and voice disorders in early untreated Parkinson's disease". *Journal of the Acoustical Society of America*,
Vol. 129, No. 1, pp. 350–367, 2011.

[Rusz 13] J. Rusz, R. Cmejla, T. Tykalova, H. Ruzickova, J. Klempir, V. Majerova,
J. Picmausova, J. Roth, and E. Ruzicka. "Imprecise vowel articulation as a
potential early marker of Parkinson's disease: effect of speaking task". *The
Journal of the Acoustical Society of America*, Vol. 134, No. 3, pp. 2171–2181,
2013.

[Saen 06] N. Sáenz-Lechón, J. I. Godino-Llorente, V. Osma-Ruiz, and P. Gómez-Vilda.
"Methodological issues in the development of automatic systems for voice
pathology detection". *Biomedical Signal Processing and Control*, Vol. 1,
pp. 120–128, 2006.

[Saka 10] C. O. Sakar and O. Kursun. "Telediagnosis of Parkinson's disease using measurements of dysphonia". *Journal of medical systems*, Vol. 34, No. 4, pp. 591–
599, 2010.

[Sapi 07] S. Sapir, J. Spielman, L. O. Ramig, B. Story, and C. Fox. "Effects of intensive
voice treatment (the Lee Silverman Voice Treatment [LSVT]) on vowel articulation in dysarthric individuals with idiopathic Parkinson disease: Acoustic
and perceptual findings". *Journal of Speech, Language, and Hearing Research*,
Vol. 50, pp. 899–912, 2007.

[Sapi 10] S. Sapir, L. O. Raming, J. L. Spielman, and C. Fox. "Formant Centralization
Ratio (FCR): a proposal for a new acoustic measure of dysarthric speech".
Journal of Speech Language and Hearing Research, Vol. 53, No. 1, pp. 1–20,
2010.

[Schl 02] M. I. Schlesinger and V. Hlavac. *Ten lectures on statistical and structural pattern recognition*. Kluwer Acadamic, Dordrecht, 2002.

[Scho 02] B. Scholköpf and A. J. Smola. *Learning with Kernel: support vector machines, regularization, optimization, and beyond*. The MIT press, Cambridge, Massachusetts, 2002.

[Schu 11] B. Schuller, A. Batliner, S. Steidl, and D. Seppi. "Recognising realistic emotions and affect in speech: State of the art and lessons learnt from the first challenge". *Speech Communication*, Vol. 53, No. 9-10, pp. 1062–1087, 2011.

[Schu 15] B. Schuller and A. Batliner. *Computational Paralinguistics: emotion, affect and personality in speech and language processing*. John Wiley & Sons, United Kingdom, 2015.

[Skod 08] S. Skodda and U. Schlegel. "Speech rate and rhythm in Parkinson's disease". *Movement disorders*, Vol. 23, No. 7, pp. 985–992, 2008.

[Skod 10] S. Skodda, A. Flasskamp, and U. Schlegel. "Instability of syllable repetition as a model for impaired motor processing: is Parkinson's disease a "rhythm disorder"?". *Journal of Neural Transmission*, Vol. 117, No. 5, pp. 605–612, May 2010.

[Skod 11a] S. Skodda, W. Grönheit, and U. Schlegel. "Gender-related patterns of dysprosody in Parkinson disease and correlation between speech variables and motor symptoms". *Journal of Voice*, Vol. 25, No. 1, pp. 76–82, 2011.

[Skod 11b] S. Skodda, W. Grönheit, and U. Schlegel. "Intonation and Speech Rate in Parkinson's Disease: General and Dynamic Aspects and Responsiveness to Levodopa Admission". *Journal of Voice*, Vol. 25, No. 4, pp. 199–205, 2011.

[Skod 11c] S. Skodda, W. Visser, and U. Schlegel. "Vowel articulation in Parkinson's diease". *Journal of Voice*, Vol. 25, No. 4, pp. 467–472, 2011. Erratum in Journal of Voice. 2012 Mar;25(2):267-8.

[Skod 12] S. Skodda, W. Grönheit, and U. Schlegel. "Impairment of vowel articulation as a possible marker of disease progression in Parkinson's disease". *PloS one*, Vol. 7, No. 2, pp. 1–8, 2012.

[Skod 13] S. Skodda, W. Grönheit, N. Mancinelli, and U. Schlegel. "Progression of voice and speech impairment in the course of Parkinson's disease: a longitudinal study". *Parkinson's Disease*, pp. 1–8, 2013.

[Slat 50] M. Slater. "Lagrange multipliers revisited". *Cowles Comission Discussion Paper: Mathematics*, No. 403, pp. 1–13, 1950.

[Sotg 13] I. Sotgiu and M. L. Rusconi. "Investigating emotions in Parkinson's disease: what we know and what we still don't know". *Frontiers in Psychology*, Vol. 4, No. June, p. 336, 2013.

[Stei 09] S. Steidl. *Automatic classification of emotion-related states in spontaneous children's speech, volume 28 of Studien zur Mustererkennung*. Logos Verlag, Berlin, Germany, 2009.

[Stev 98] K. N. Stevens. *Acoustic Phonetics*. The MIT Press, Cambridge, 1998.

[Sun 10]   Y. Sun, S. Todorovic, and S. Goodison. "Local learning based feature selection for high dimensional data analysis". *IEEE Transactions on Pattern Analysis and Machine Intelligence*, Vol. 32, No. 9, pp. 1610–1626, 2010.

[Take 81] F. Takens. "Detecting strange attractors in turbulence". *Dynamical Systems and Turbulence: Lecture Notes in Mathematics*, Vol. 898, pp. 366–381, 1981.

[Tsan 10a] A. Tsanas, M. A. Little, P. E. McSharry, and L. O. Ramig. "Accurate telemonitoring of Parkinson's disease progression by noninvasive speech tests". *IEEE Transactions on Biomedical Engineering*, Vol. 57, No. 4, pp. 884–893, 2010.

[Tsan 10b] A. Tsanas, M. Little, P. McSharry, and L. Ramig. "Nonlinear speech analysis algorithms mapped to a standard metric achieve clinically useful quantification of average Parkinson's disease symptom severity". *Journal of the Royal Society, Interface / the Royal Society*, Vol. 8, No. 59, pp. 842–855, 2010.

[Tsan 11] A. Tsanas, M. A. Little, P. E. Mcsharry, and L. O. Ramig. "Nonlinear speech analysis algorithms mapped to a standard metric achieve clinically useful quantification of average Parkinson's disease symptom severity". *Journal of the Royal Society Interface*, Vol. 8, No. 59, pp. 842–855, 2011.

[Tsan 12] A. Tsanas, M. Little, P. Mcsharry, J. Spielman, and L. Ramig. "Novel speech signal processing algorithms for high-accuracy classification of Parkinson's Disease". *IEEE Transactions on Biomedical Engineering*, Vol. 59, No. 5, pp. 1264–1271, 2012.

[Tsan 14] A. Tsanas, M. Little, C. Fox, and L. Ramig. "Objective automatic assessment of rehabilitative speech treatment in Parkinson's disease". *IEEE Transactions on Neural Systems and Rehabilitation Engineering*, Vol. 22, No. 1, pp. 181–190, 2014.

[Turn 95] G. Turner, Tjaden, and G. Weismer. "The influence of speaking rate on vowel space and speech intelligibility for individuals with Amyotrophic Lateral Sclerosis". *Journal of Speech and Hearing Research*, Vol. 38, No. , pp. 1001–1013, 1995.

[Tyka 14] T. Tykalova, J. Rusz, R. Cmejla, H. Ruzickova, and E. Ruzicka. "Acoustic investigation of stress patterns in Parkinson's disease". *Journal of voice*, Vol. 28, No. 1, pp. 129.e1–129.e8, 2014.

[Tyka 15] T. Tykalová, J. Rusz, R. Čmejla, J. Klempíř, H. Růžičková, J. Roth, and E. Růžička. "Effect of dopaminergic medication on speech dysfluency in Parkinson's disease: a longitudinal study". *Journal of Neural Transmission*, 2015.

[Vapn 95] V. Vapnik. *The nature of statistical learning theory*. Springer-Verlag, New York, 1995.

[Vasq 14] J. C. Vásquez-Correa, J. R. Orozco-Arroyave, J. D. Arias-Londoño, J. F. Vargas-Bonilla, and E. Nöth. "New computer aided device for real time analysis of speech of people with Parkinson's disease". *Revista Facultad de Ingeniería Universidad de Antioquia*, Vol. 1, No. 72, pp. 87–103, 2014.

[Vasq 15] J. C. Vásquez-Correa, T. Arias-Vergara, J. R. Orozco-Arroyave, J. D. Arias-Londoño, J. F. Vargas-Bonilla, and E. Nöth. "Automatic detection of Parkinson's disease from continuous speech recorded in non-controlled noise conditions". In: *Proceedings of the 16th Annual Conference of the International Speech Communication Association (INTERSPEECH)*, Dresden, Germany, 2015.

[Vija 07] P. Vijayalakshmi, M. R. Reddy, and D. O'Shaughnessy. "Acoustic analysis and detection of hypernasality using a group delay function". *Transactions on Biomedical Engineering*, Vol. 54, No. 4, pp. 621–629, 2007.

[Vire 11]   M. Virebrand. *Real-time monitoring of voice characteristics using accelero-meter and microphone measurements*. Master Thesis, Linköpings Universitet, Department of Electrical Engineering, Linköping, Sweden, June 2011.

[Wahl 06]   W. Wahlser, Ed. *SmartKom: foundations of multimodal dialogue systems*. Springer-Verlag, Berlin, Germany, 2006.

[Wals 11]   B. Walsh and A. Smith. "Linguistic complexity, speech production, and comprehension in Parkinson's disease: behavioral and physiological indices". *Journal of Speech, Language, and Hearing Research*, Vol. 54, No. June, pp. 787–803, 2011.

[Wang 05]   Y. T. Wang, R. D. Kent, J. R. Duffy, and J. E. Thomas. "Dysarthria associated with traumatic brain injury: Speaking rate and emphatic stress". *Journal of Communication Disorders*, Vol. 38, No. 3, pp. 231–260, 2005.

[Wats 08]   P. J. Watson and B. Munson. "Parkinson's disease and the effect of lexical factors on vowel articulation". *The Journal of the Acoustical Society of America*, Vol. 124, No. 5, pp. EL291–EL295, 2008.

[Weis 84]   G. Weismer. "Articulatory characteristics of Parkinsonian dysarthria: deg-mental and phrase-level timing, spirantization, and glottal coordination". In: *The dysarthrias: physiology, acoustics, perception, management*, pp. 101–130, College-Hill Press, 1984.

[Weis 88]   G. Weismer, R. Kent, M. Hodge, and R. Martin. "The acoustic signature for intelligibility test words". *Journal of the Acoustic Society of America*, No. 84, pp. 1281–1291, 1988.

[Wolf 61]   P. Wolfe. "A duality theorem for non-linear programming". *Quarterly of Applied Mathematics*, No. 19, pp. 239–244, 1961.

[Wort 13]   P. Worth. "How to treat Parkinson's disease in 2013". *Clinical Medicine*, Vol. 13, No. 1, pp. 93–96, 2013.

[Xu 05]   L. S. Xu, K. Wang, and L. Wang. "Gaussian kernel approximate entropy al-gorithm for analyzing irregularity of time series". In: *Proceedings of the Inter-national Conference on Machine Learning and Cybernetics*, pp. 5605–5608, 2005.

[Yumo 82]   E. Yumoto, W. Gould, and T. Baer. "Harmonics-to-noise ratio as an index of the degree of hoarseness". *Journal of the Acoustical Society of America*, Vol. 71, No. 6, pp. 1544–1550, 1982.

[Zeis 06]   V. Zeißler, J. Adelhardt, A. Batliner, C. Frank, E. Nöth, R. Shi, and H. Niemann. "The Prosody Module". In: *SmartKom: Foundations of Mul-timodal Dialogue Systems*, pp. 139–152, Springer, 2006.

[Zick 80]   J. E. Zicker, W. J. Tompkins, R. T. Rubow, and J. H. Abbs. "A portable microprocessor-based bio-feedback training device". *IEEE Transactions on Biomedical Engineering*, No. 9, pp. 509–515, 1980.

[Zwic 57]   E. Zwicker, G. Flottorp, and S. S. Stevens. "Critical band width in loudness summation". *The Journal of the Acoustical Society of America*, Vol. 29, No. 5, pp. 548–557, 1957.

[Zwic 80]   E. Zwicker and E. Terhardt. "Analytical expressions for critical-band rate and critical bandwidth as a function of frequency". *Journal of the Acoustical Soci-ety of America*, Vol. 68, No. 5, pp. 1523–1525, 1980.

In der Reihe *Studien zur Mustererkennung,*

herausgegeben von

Prof. Dr. Ing Heinricht Niemann und Herrn Prof. Dr. Ing. Elmar Nöth

sind bisher erschienen:

1	Jürgen Haas	Probabilistic Methods in Linguistic Analysis
		ISBN 978-3-89722-565-7, 2000, 260 S. 40.50 €
2	Manuela Boros	Partielles robustes Parsing spontansprachlicher Dialoge am Beispiel von Zugauskunftdialogen
		ISBN 978-3-89722-600-5, 2001, 264 S. 40.50 €
3	Stefan Harbeck	Automatische Verfahren zur Sprachdetektion, Landessprachenerkennung und Themendetektion
		ISBN 978-3-89722-766-8, 2001, 260 S. 40.50 €
4	Julia Fischer	Ein echtzeitfähiges Dialogsystem mit iterativer Ergebnisoptimierung
		ISBN 978-3-89722-867-2, 2002, 222 S. 40.50 €
5	Ulrike Ahlrichs	Wissensbasierte Szenenexploration auf der Basis erlernter Analysestrategien
		ISBN 978-3-89722-904-4, 2002, 165 S. 40.50 €
6	Florian Gallwitz	Integrated Stochastic Models for Spontaneous Speech Recognition
		ISBN 978-3-89722-907-5, 2002, 196 S. 40.50 €
7	Uwe Ohler	Computational Promoter Recognition in Eukaryotic Genomic DNA
		ISBN 978-3-89722-988-4, 2002, 206 S. 40.50 €
8	Richard Huber	Prosodisch-linguistische Klassifikation von Emotion
		ISBN 978-3-89722-984-6, 2002, 293 S. 40.50 €

29	Andreas Maier	Speech of Children with Cleft Lip and Palate: Automatic Assessment
		ISBN 978-3-8325-2144-8, 2009, 220 S. 37.00 €
30	Christian Hacker	Automatic Assessment of Children Speech to Support Language Learning
		ISBN 978-3-8325-2258-2, 2009, 272 S. 39.00 €
31	Jan-Henning Trustorff	Der Einsatz von Support Vector Machines zur Kreditwürdigkeitsbeurteilung von Unternehmen
		ISBN 978-3-8325-2375-6, 2009, 260 S. 38.00 €
32	Martin Raab	Real World Approaches for Multilingual and Non-native Speech Recognition
		ISBN 978-3-8325-2446-3, 2010, 168 S. 44.00 €
33	Michael Wels	Probabilistic Modeling for Segmentation in Magnetic Resonance Images of the Human Brain
		ISBN 978-3-8325-2631-3, 2010, 148 S. 40.00 €
34	Florian Jäger	Normalization of Magnetic Resonance Images and its Application to the Diagnosis of the Scoliotic Spine
		ISBN 978-3-8325-2779-2, 2011, 168 S. 36.00 €
35	Viktor Zeißler	Robuste Erkennung der prosodischen Phänomene und der emotionalen Benutzerzustände in einem multimodalen Dialogsystem
		ISBN 978-3-8325-3167-6, 2012, 380 S. 43.50 €
36	Korbinian Riedhammer	Interactive Approaches to Video Lecture Assessment
		ISBN 978-3-8325-3235-2, 2012, 164 S. 40.50 €
37	Stefan Wenhardt	Ansichtenauswahl für die 3-D-Rekonstruktion statischer Szenen
		ISBN 978-3-8325-3465-3, 2013, 218 S. 37.00 €
38	Kerstin Müller	3-D Imaging of the Heart Chambers with C-arm CT
		ISBN 978-3-8325-3726-5, 2014, 174 S. 46.00 €

39	Chen Li	Content-based Microscopic Image Analysis
		ISBN 978-3-8325-4253-5, 2016, 196 S. 36.50 €
40	Christian Feinen	Object Representation and Matching Based on Skeletons and Curves
		ISBN 978-3-8325-4257-3, 2016, 260 S. 50.50 €
41	Juan Rafael Orozco-Arroyave	Analysis of Speech of People with Parkinson's Disease
		ISBN 978-3-8325-4361-7, 2016, 138 S. 38.00 €

Alle erschienenen Bücher können unter der angegebenen ISBN im Buchhandel oder direkt beim Logos Verlag Berlin (www.logos-verlag.de, Fax: 030 - 42 85 10 92) bestellt werden.